D0174230

BRETHREN,
HANG
LOOSE

ALSO BY ROBERT GIRARD

Brethren, Hang Together

My Weakness . . . His Strength

OR WHAT'S HAPPENING TO MY CHURCH?

ROBERT C. GIRARD

Introduction by Lawrence O. Richards

BRETHREN, HANG LOOSE!

Grand Rapids, Michigan

ISBN 0-310-25041-2

Library of Congress Catalog Card Number 77-183050

Printed in the United States of America

83 84 85 86 87 88 — 20 19 18 17

To
the people of Our Heritage,
whose openness and love
gave me an opportunity to see
JESUS CHRIST
alive in His Church.

CONTENTS

PREFACE

This is not a "success story." Horatio Alger wouldn't touch it with a ten foot pole. And it wouldn't make very good reading in a denominational magazine either.

I have told this story to ministerial colleagues and have become very accustomed to the question: "Since you've started this 'new approach' to the ministry has your church grown?" (They *always* mean numerically). And my answer always has to be "no." Because, after just three years of moving toward church renewal, and toward what I hope is the New Testament ideal for church life, the best I can report is that attendance on Sunday morning is *noticeably* down! My ego hastens to point out a 2000 percent increase in people involved in mid-week Bible study, and two new congregations in other parts of the city to which we have given "mothering" and members. But statistical boasting about our own church is quite subdued by statistical realities.

But . . . for the *first time* in my ministerial life I'm enjoying being a pastor. For the first time in my relationship with the church (a lifelong relationship) I'm seeing . . . and *experiencing* . . . LIFE!

And I wouldn't trade it for all the statistics of St. Peter's of Rome!

This is also an *unfinished* story. Whatever we are experiencing is no more than the *beginning* of renewal. "The Acts of the Apostles" isn't yet being relived at Our Heritage Church.

However . . . We *are* beginning to smell its fragrance. Around the edges of our fellowship an occasional glimpse of New Testament life becomes visible. Enough so that we can imagine now, what it will be like when Christ is given freedom to do in and through us *all* He came to do.

I did not plan to write a book.

But through a rather amazing set of circumstances, my wife, Audrey, and I found ourselves in Minneapolis attending the *Decision* Magazine School of Christian Writing. *Somehow* we were able to get in, in spite of the fact that by the time we applied, they were no longer accepting registrants, and in spite of the fact that there was no time for us to submit the usually-required sample of our writing. Beside this, our expenses were paid.

Six weeks later, I was sitting in a lawn chair beside a swimming pool in Scottsdale, chatting with friend Larry Richards. We were talking about church renewal and what God was doing at Our Heritage.

Suddenly, Larry was saying, "Why don't you write a book?"

And I was saying, "It's too soon. Give us another five years."

"It's needed *now,*" Larry replied. "You can write a sequel in five years if you want to."

"I don't know if I could write a book," I said.

But five days later I was knocking at his apartment door with a preliminary outline for this book.

His encouragement, and that of Bob DeVries of Zondervan, kept me going several times when I wondered if I wasn't kidding myself thinking I could write anything this big.

During this writing, I have continued to serve the wonderful and understanding congregation of Our Heritage Wesleyan Church as pastor. It is extremely doubtful that I could have finished the job without the encouragement they gave me. Several times when I was about to "throw in the sponge," individuals and groups in the church assured me they were praying for my writing.

Mary Lazear came to me in the Spirit, more than once, to rebuke me in love for my neglect of this project in order to give my time to something far down the priority scale.

The leaders of the church enthusiastically granted the extra time away necessary to do the last few chapters.

Sammy Statini gave hours and hours to the task of typing the manuscript. Hap Wysocki prepared the pages and pages of Xerox copies. These ladies produced a beautiful manuscript — one I was proud to send to the publisher.

Carl Jackson, my dearest friend who lived this with me, helped jog near-forgotten details from my sluggish memory, and, by his own sensitivity to the Spirit, he provided the contents of an entire chapter about his unique Circle Church.

My editor was my extremely patient wife and counselor, Audrey. The book would be many pages longer without her careful cutting of my unnecessary repetitions and detours into sassy rhetoric on some pet peeve. She constantly encouraged me and helped to create an atmosphere for writing.

Because of her enthusiasm for this project, the kids — Christine, 16; Bobby, 8; and Charity Joy, 18 months — understood why Dad was not as available as he might have been on his "day off."

My prayer, as I share this with whoever reads it, is that the activity of the Living Spirit of Christ will be seen in and through the whole story. I hope that clearly visible will be the Spirit's beautiful knack for using circumstances, frustrations, reverses, unsolved problems, and His Word injected at strategic moments. For the naked truth is, that we would still be struggling on, stale and unchanged, frustrated and dissatisfied, were it not for His faithful and loving maneuvering to back us into a corner again and again, where there was little else to do but to listen to Him.

I pray that the Holy Spirit will use this story to stimulate the kind of heart-searching, honesty, openness, and surrender that can lead toward new life in the church. But at the same time, I also pray that no one will be so foolish as to look to this feeble, human effort as a manual for renewal. *The New Testament* is the one and only reliable *manual for renewal*. If its teaching concerning the Church is confronted with a really open mind [illegible] one depending on the Spirit who wrote it, the keys to renewal will all be discovered just lying there, unused, untapped, in its exciting pages.

ROBERT C. GIRARD

Scottsdale, Arizona

INTRODUCTION

Hang loose?

This book is misnamed! It should be called, "Take Heart." For that's what God's message through Bob Girard is. To everyone who has looked into the Bible and seen Christ's Church on earth, then looked in dismay at his own church and seen the gap between the two — to everyone who has become aware of the church God's Word invites us to become and the church so many of us experience . . . Take heart! God is alive and well and ready to *act* in our lives and in our fellowships.

This is a great message for us today — especially from a pastor like Bob Girard, who didn't move out to start an "experimental work" but, staying with a church like yours and mine, led it to change. This excites me, because I believe that today's churches do not deserve abandonment but desperately do need to recapture the freedom of the Spirit to change, and to become what God intends them to be. Bob Girard experienced frustration, but he didn't abandon his charge. Pastor Bob found grace to trust God, and wisdom to lead His people in change.

Bob Girard tells an unfinished story in this book because God is still at work among the people of Our Heritage Church. God is still creating, still building, still changing, as pastor and church alike struggle to keep themselves open to His leading. Bob tells it like it is — honestly sharing the problems and difficulties which steps toward renewal bring. But with it he shows us all how exciting and vital and fresh life in Christ can be as His people accept the Divine invitation to live together as the Body of Christ, the family "in Christ," that they are.

Today a host of books and articles have made us increasingly aware of our failures and needs in the church. And some have begun to guide us toward the open door of renewal — the invitation to reconstruct our fellowship on Biblical principles and patterns. And now we hear from Bob Girard, *a man who has gone through that open door!* And what he shares is compelling evidence that there is new life for your church and for mine if we'll only take heart, trust God, and *act,* guided by His Spirit.

Hang loose, Bob. We're almost ready to hang in there with you!

Thanks so much for pointing the way.

LAWRENCE O. RICHARDS

Wheaton College,
Wheaton, Illinois

BRETHREN,
HANG
LOOSE

1

THE GLORIOUS EVANGELICAL STATUS QUO

"WHAT'S HAPPENING to my church?" I moaned.

The four of us: my wife Audrey, Associate Pastor Carl Jackson, his wife Ann, and I sat in a furrow-browed little huddle in the parsonage living room. It was Sunday night. We'd just shut off the last lights at the church and driven in gloomy silence to the house to try to regroup after a congregational business meeting that had fallen in around us!

The meeting had been called to consider the purchase of a second parsonage for the associate pastor. We'd had the creeping feeling for several weeks that "the honeymoon was over" in our new church. Tonight we were sure of it!

The meeting was tense from the start. It soon degenerated into an exchange of emotion-charged suspicions, at the height of which one of our leading laymen grabbed his wife by the hand and stalked out in frustration and anger!

We prayed and claimed Romans 8:28 and told each other we were trusting. But to me it was like sounding the "death knell" on all the hopes and dreams I had held for this new church since its first services two and one-half years before.

I had honestly thought that if I could start my own new church ("pioneering" we call it) I could keep it free from some of the things I saw wrong in the established institutional churches.

But after a "very successful" two years, in spite of the fact that it was a new church in a new community and was composed of new Christians, we now discovered rather abruptly that

Our Heritage was rapidly developing some of the same old institutional diseases we had naively thought we could avoid, simply by starting a new church with a few new ideas.

We discovered in a matter of a few weeks, climaxing with the aforesaid business meeting disaster, that we were settling down to becoming a typical, average, everyday, run-of-the-mill, carnal evangelical congregation. And not only were we plagued with suspicion, mistrust and jealousy, but as we now began to examine ourselves, our spiritual immaturity showed up everywhere in the life of the church.

For instance . . . I preached regularly about Christian witnessing, and a significant number of our members had received training at Campus Crusade for Christ Lay Institutes on how to share their faith. But only a few regularly talked to other people about Christ.

I preached about prayer. We tried to get people together for prayer meetings. The results were depressing. My wife, Audrey, who never says "Amen," but keeps praying all day long, says that knowing we were nearly alone in the "prayer-battle" was to her the most crushing burden of all. And to our knowledge, almost no one prayed.

We had pot-luck suppers, ice cream socials, "coffee and chatter" after the services. There were Sunday school parties, youth parties, adult parties, children's parties. Our people exchanged "friendship cards" in the worship services. We provided greeters at the door, formed a "Fishermen's Club" to call on newcomers. We bowled together, played golf together, went to ball games together. And we went to church three times a week together. But still our experience of fellowship went little deeper than "What do you think of the heat?"

We worked. Often for two or three months straight I would average eighteen hours a day on the job. And it seemed as if nothing would move unless I pushed it! (I guess I should have been happy it moved when I pushed. I've been in pastoral situations where that definitely was not the story. You could push your heart out and the whole church just laid there — an immovable, implacable heap of solid granite!) The congregation, the program, the evangelism, the life of the church all seemed too overwhelmingly dependent on the pastors.

And I had the awful feeling that if anything happened to Carl and me or to the church building, the whole thing would disintegrate before our eyes!

Call it arrogance or stupidity – perhaps it was both – but I felt that way. I felt that we were a bunch of babies in Christ and it looked as if there was little hope we'd ever be anything else.

We were beginning to experience "The Glorious Evangelical Status Quo"!

And furthermore, we were at a total loss to know what to do about it!

After all, we had everything you're supposed to have to be a vital, evangelical, Bible-believing church. Sunday school (*two* of them). Worship service (again, *two*). Sunday evening service. Prayer group (?). Youth groups. Choirs (*five!*) Pastors (two of them – good ones). Sunday bulletin. Midweek reminder. Bible-centered Sunday school literature. We had it all!

And we were growing. After two and one-half years our Sunday school was hitting 250 regularly. As a result of our ministry, nearly 200 people had personally prayed to receive Christ. More than 100 had joined the church. Ninety percent of our church members had come to Christ through the ministry of our new church.

By all the usual standards that are applied to determine church success – we were a success!

(And I loved the accolades of my fellow evangelicals and the leaders of my denomination. *Ah, at last, I am a "success"!*)

But success was mingled with the bitter taste of disappointment, as I tried to reassemble my dreams and hopes after that "cold" night in September, when at a business meeting we saw ourselves as we *really* were.

How It All Started

On February 25, 1965, Audrey and I with our children had arrived in the land of sunshine and cactus, full of hopes and high on sheer excitement mingled with fear.

I had been in the ministry for twelve years. Much of that time I had spent trying desperately to find out where I fit, what I was supposed to be doing, and what the church was supposed to be doing. (I'm not sure any of these questions was really answered by the time we arrived in Arizona.)

Four pastorates in six years for four different denominations. Then for five years God allowed me to escape the pastorate and find a new niche for myself on the public relations and fund-raising staff of our church college. (Many times I fought the urge to go *back* to the pastorate.)

One year in the motion picture ministry of the Billy Graham Evangelistic Association. Exciting – the big crowds, the impressive accumulation of statistics on "decisions for Christ." But there was something in me that wanted and needed to do more than just sweep into town, "evangelize" a large crowd, count converts, and then sweep out, leaving the spiritual development of these new converts to someone else.

The thought of going back to pastor an established church left me feeling very uncertain and afraid. I remembered too well my past pastoral experiences.

There were things that bothered me deeply about the established churches – not only those of my own denomination, but evangelical churches in general. And the better I came to know the church and the longer I worked with it, the more bothered I became.

When I read *The Acts of the Apostles* and compared it with nearly all the churches I had ever known, I felt frustrated, hopeless and a little sick.

That dynamic New Testament church effectively communicated Christ to its generation. Most of the church, as I knew it, wasn't even *really* concerned about that. It was too busy with other things.

That church was characterized by love for one another that was so real, even the world knew about it. Most churches and Christians I had known (there were exceptions) knew nothing of that kind of love. Rather, one church I had pastored, was known county-wide for feuding among its members. One of its charter members told me one day, "I've never liked any pastor we've ever had. And you're no exception!" And she meant it.

Spirituality was being equated with rules and man-made standards. A woman's spirituality was judged by the length of her skirts or how much make-up she did or didn't wear. A man was "spiritual" if he didn't smoke, didn't drink, didn't play cards or shoot pool, didn't go to movies, didn't say "darn," paid his tithe, was endlessly busy on church committees. His life didn't really have to produce anything of witness in the outside world or love within the Body of believers. He could indulge in all sorts of sins of attitude and desire, and as long as he refused to "taste, touch or handle" the specified "no-no's," he could hob-nob with the spiritually elite in the church.

In the church as I knew it, a pastor was a "success" if his Sunday school attendance and membership increased by ten percent, if his offerings were better than last year, if he received annual salary raises, if his wife was well-liked, if he was elected to office in the local ministerial association, if he was able to keep the Women's Missionary Society happy, and if he could keep his major contributors reasonably well "buttered up." If he could do all these important things he was certain to be considered for a bigger and better church and possibly for a strategic office in the district organization. This was the *sure* sign that he had been recognized as a "success."

The whole world was living in the space age — talking about rocket trips to the planets. But the church as I knew it and its leaders were smugly, self-righteously satisfied to be seeking to reach a generation that had died before the airplane was invented.

I hated these things about the church.

I hated its smallness of vision, its suspicion and jealousy of the few men who succeeded in really reaching people, its fear of anything fresh and new, its bondage to clichés, its stuff-shirted spiritual pride, its power politics (which it always tried to hide behind a facade of piety), its endless reports of nothing happening, its press releases that glossed over its failures.

I deplored its total unwillingness to change. Its unwillingness to be honest about its own failures and sins. Its utter inability to drop a method or a practice or a program that was not working to try to find a better way.

I despised the red tape, the unwieldy, super-slow movement of its governmental bodies. I was convinced that if the Holy Spirit did want to do something different or dynamic – He'd lose heart trying to get through all the committees and boards that would have to approve it!

And yet . . . while I hated and despised it all – I was a tin-plate *hypocrite!* For I'd have given my Memory-o-Matic filing system for a place of leadership in the administrative echelons of my denomination's tower of red tape. And I was using some of the same standards I was condemning to measure the success of my ministry. I was deeply involved in the political machinery, the shallow value scales, and the public relations cover-ups. I had my own set of legalistic requirements by which I measured other people's spirituality. I was jealous of pastors of the "big churches" and envious of those who were elected to district and denominational offices. And in my very "honesty" about the church's failures and weaknesses I was guilty of my own brand of spiritual pride.

But, somehow, I thought if I could start my own church I could keep it free from some of the things I saw wrong in the established institutional churches.

I believe, sincerely, we were led by the Spirit of God to move to Scottsdale, Arizona, to begin the church that had already been named "Our Heritage Wesleyan Methodist Church." It was a lot more than disdain for the failures of the established churches that brought us here. Those things may have influenced and heightened our desire to start a new church instead of pastoring an old one, but it was the positive challenge that most deeply motivated us.

I must admit, when I think of what my denomination was willing to do to start a new congregation in Scottsdale, there certainly was no smallness of vision demonstrated on the part of the men who planned this venture. It was a far cry from many of the pioneering ventures I'd heard about. No store-front church here. No rented facilities. No holding down two jobs to support myself. Nothing that I felt I needed was denied me. An attractive building in the heart of a booming suburban housing area. A home, salary and adequate money for advertising, office equipment, etc.

As I've taken visiting ministers through the lovely buildings, shown them the rheostat lighting, the soft carpeting and the padded pews, with tongue-in-cheek I've said, "*This* is what I call 'pioneering'!"

In addition to substantially underwriting the Our Heritage venture, my ecclesiastical leaders gave me one important thing that cleared the way for some of the new things I'll be telling you about in this book.

They gave me *freedom.*

From the very beginning I have had freedom to do whatever I felt should be done to build the church. I was told by one official that the sponsoring district wanted to see people coming to Christ in Scottsdale and that I would be free to use *any* means I felt appropriate to make this happen.[1]

And as we began preparations for the move to Arizona, the Spirit gave Audrey a promise that we have both clung to these five years — a promise of a renewed church — a promise we have not fully understood until now:

> "I will go before thee, and make the crooked paths straight, and the dark places light" (Isaiah).

(We have quoted this all these years, but not until beginning to write this book did we realize that it was a misquote. You have to combine Isaiah 40:4 and 42:16 to come up with "our" promise.)

There was a prayer I prayed again and again during the days before the church began and throughout its early development: "Lord, please build a New Testament Church in Scottsdale."

I hardly knew what I was saying. I really had no idea what a "New Testament Church" would be like. I thought of a witnessing church, an evangelistic church, a church which recognized the Holy Spirit. But my concept of a "New Testament Church" went little further than that. I can remember admitting,

[1] 1 Corinthians 9:22.

as I talked to God about it, that I wasn't sure what I was asking for. So, in our praying, we would add: "Lord, build it *Your* way. Build *Your* kind of church here. *Whatever* that means!"

And . . . the Lord began to build it – *His* way.

A Church for Non-Christians

From the beginning we made up our minds that we would not seek to build a church to attract Christians. We felt God had brought us here to reach the uncommitted, the pagan.

Four basic ideas became our "code" for reaching this purpose:

(1) Accept people where they are.
(2) If changes are needed in their lives, let the Holy Spirit do it.
(3) Avoid the old evangelical cliches like the plague.
(4) Program to the hilt.

Accept people where they are. If people with *any* bad habit, *any* questionable occupation, *any* way-out philosophy, *any* political persuasion, *any* kind of life-style were willing to listen to me preach or associate in any way with the church, we made up our minds ahead of time that we would accept them and love them and seek to introduce them to Christ just as they are. We would not ask them to change *anything* in order to have our ministry or to be accepted into our congregation. All would be treated alike as far as it was humanly possible.

We made up our minds ahead of time that no one who loved the Lord Jesus Christ would be refused membership in the church. We refused to lay unscriptural requirements on people who wanted to unite with us. [2]

If changes are needed in their lives, let the Holy Spirit do it. When we try to legislate and coerce people to accept certain outward standards of behavior which we think will make them "more spiritual," we are robbing them of some very precious experiences with the living Lord Himself. We are putting them into man-made "boxes," hemming them in spiritually, and stealing from them the beautiful experience of freedom to be personally led and taught by the Holy Spirit and the Word.

[2] 1 Corinthians 10:23; 12:3; Colossians 2:20-23 (Amplified).

When we get another believer to adjust his life to fit our moldy little molds, it's great for our own egos — but does nearly irreparable damage to that Christian's personal relationship to "the law of the Spirit of life in Christ Jesus" (Romans 8:2). By imposing our own conscience on him, we kill in him some of the vitality and life of the Spirit (2 Corinthians 3:6). And the exciting person-to-Person aspect of his relationship with Christ is depersonalized. The abundant Christian life is reduced to the drudgery of a set of lifeless rules!

One of our growing new Christians had been reading an evangelical magazine and ran across a little article about dancing. Within minutes the parsonage phone was ringing. Audrey answered. The lady on the line immediately asked, "Is it really wrong for a Christian to dance?"

She was a little chagrined when Audrey refused a direct answer. "Look," Audrey told her, "I know it would be easy for both of us if I just answered 'yes' or 'no.' But that wouldn't help you to learn how to walk in the Spirit. It would only impose my convictions on you. If all you want is a set of rules, you might as well be a Moslem. If you are honestly willing to do what God wants you to do in this area of your life, you can pray about it, read your Bible (Audrey listed one or two appropriate passages for her to read) and the *Holy Spirit* will show you what *His* answer is." She did and He did.

The same approach was taken on many other such issues. And, while not every person has come to the same conclusions, they have learned that it is the Spirit of God speaking through His Word — *not* the pastor or the church's high councils — who is responsible and able to lead them in the nitty-gritty of everyday life.

Avoid the old evangelical cliches like the plague. We determined ahead of opening day that it would not be necessary for a man to be able to converse or listen in King James English to hear the Gospel, believe and be "saved." Instead of expecting the pagan to learn a new vocabulary, the Christian witness must understand his own message well enough to put it into terms even the uninitiated and completely unchurched can comprehend.

The preaching and teaching at Our Heritage, we decided, would find new ways to say it.

Some words we evangelicals throw around without a thought are not only not understood by the average American pagan, they are actually *mis*understood. They conjure up ideas of emotional excesses, weird practices, and experiences with "some 'Christian' I knew when I was a kid" – experiences that have helped to "turn me off on 'religion.' "

"Revival" is such a word. Its real meaning is obscured by mental images of people rolling in the aisles, loud praying, and other practices that have made some churches a laughingstock.

"Getting saved" is almost universally equated with long, emotional appeals to "get right with God," death-bed stories, "hell-fire and damnation" and a "trip to the altar."

"Repentance" is either a public display of weeping, or a decision to quit smoking or drinking or playing cards and start going to church.

Other terms are simply totally meaningless – useless in communicating to the man who hasn't been exposed to evangelicalism, the Bible or the usual conservative Christian modus operandi.

Instead of calling men to "get saved" or "get religion," we spoke of "an encounter with Christ" . . . "forgiveness for attitudes and acts of self-will and independence from God." Instead of shouting "Repent!" (which is all right if you've explained to the pagan what the word means and what he is to repent of), we spoke of "turning from self-rule to Christ's control." Instead of pointing our finger and saying "You're lost! You need to be saved," we tried to show the pagan "the emptiness of a man's life without Christ," his "separation from God" . . . "the God-shaped vacuum in every man that only Christ can fill" (Pascal). Instead of talking to new believers about their need for "Pentecost" . . . "holiness" . . . "sanctification," we taught them what the Bible means when it speaks of being "filled (controlled) with the Spirit."

We sometimes use the old terms – at least those that are biblical – but try to make it clear to those who hear what we are talking about. Trying to preach and teach dependence on the "old cliches" is hard work. Trying to say it differently, in language the uninitiated can understand, has forced me to face the fact that in my prior use of a lot of those grand old phrases, I really didn't know what I was talking about. I'm a better Christian today because I've had to find out what I was saying before I said it. In fact, it was so helpful to my own understanding of the Gospel that I constantly press our people to explain *their* use of terms, lest they be rendered ineffective in their day-to-day witnessing and their own understanding of the Gospel by leaning too heavily on language the meaning of which has slipped away.

With this in mind, we also did some other things that seemed strange to evangelicals who visited our services in those early days. We provided Bibles in the pews, instead of de-spiritualizing people who didn't bring their own. And passages to be read for responsive readings and as sermon texts were announced both by reference *and by page number*.

All of these things, and our acceptance of everyone who came, made us unacceptable to many evangelical Christians. Dozens joined our "awakening pagans" for worship and then promptly tuned us out, suddenly turning up in some other evangelical church. Desperately needed Christian lay leadership came and left like the tide, without pausing long enough to look deeper — not wanting to get involved.

One typical comment came from a talented Christian family of our own denomination who, upon moving to town, attended our services a few times with their teenage daughters. They shortly decided to become part of another church because "there are too many unsaved kids in your youth group and we're afraid of their influence on our daughters."

This was a story repeated again and again. Only the names and age-level were changed to fit the individual situation.

It was difficult to understand at first. Then we remembered our prayer that He build His church His way. And we began to thank Him as He taught us to stop depending on people (especially "Christians"), and to depend *only* on Him.

Program to the hilt. I've already described some of this earlier (see page 19). I honestly had the idea that the church lights should be burning every night of the week. It didn't occur to me that any family who participated in all that was happening at the church would be tragically splintered — almost never together as a family. It never entered my institutional brain that if everyone participated in everything in which I was expecting them to participate they could not possibly involve themselves as witnesses in community life or in the lives of their neighbors. These revelations didn't come until after God's "shock treatment" at that fateful business meeting in September, 1967.

It cannot be denied, however, that the Lord used the early emphasis on programming to bring pagans to faith in Christ and into the church.

But all our programming could not bring about spiritual maturity. It seemed, rather, to encourage dependence on "the program." And it couldn't prevent the development of many of the old institutional diseases. Those diseases became quite visible on that "cold" night in September.

And Carl and I began to ask, "Is this *really* the task we've been called to do: to build a large congregation of new Christians . . . and then just try to keep these spiritual babies dry and happy 'til Jesus comes?

"Or is there more to building a church?"

11

THE BIGGEST ROADBLOCK TO RENEWAL

"More?

"What *more* could I possibly do? Lord, I'm already working harder and longer than any pastor I know! I'm in this thing day and night.

"You *know* what my priority list looks like:

The church first — *always.*

My family second — *always.*

"How can I possibly improve on that?

"No church in town has more going than we do. Everything that is supposed to make us a vital, living, Bible-believing, evangelistic church is being done. I'm trying — *really trying* — to be faithful, to fulfill the Great Commission, to reach Scottsdale for Christ, to build a New Testament Church.

"But, Lord, something is wrong! It's not happening. Our attendance and membership are increasing. People are praying to receive Christ. But we can't seem to get them beyond that. We can't seem to grow out of our spiritual babyhood.

"Much of what is happening is *no miracle* at all. It can be explained so easily: When I work, it goes. When I don't, *nothing* happens! Everything can be explained in terms of human effort.

"Where is the divine life the New Testament Church had? What *more* do *I* have to *do* to make it happen here?"

That's how I found myself talking to God.

It came out differently when I talked to my wife on those

super-tense Friday and Saturday nights when she would talk to me about trusting the Lord and about taking some time to rest. I was so tied in knots by the load I was trying to carry "all by myself" that there were times when "climbing the walls" was literally what I found myself trying to do.

"You've got to leave it to the Lord," she would say.

"*Leave it to the Lord*? Will the Lord mimeograph the bulletin, sing the solo, teach the Sunday school class and contact the families who need to be contacted before Sunday? Will the Lord write my sermon, prepare my Sunday school lesson and meet Mrs. So-and-so for counseling? Will the Lord see to it that the lawn is mowed and the janitor work is done right? Will the Lord recruit those substitute teachers we need for tomorrow morning and deliver the materials to them tonight? Will the Lord run down to the newspaper office with these news releases? Will the Lord go on the air for my Sunday morning radio broadcast?

"If I don't do it, *nobody* will!"

Or, in my more desperate moments, when mind and body cried out to be free from the pressure for even a little while: "God doesn't care about how much work I have to do! He sent us down here to Scottsdale – told us to win these people to Christ – but He left all the work for *me* to do! I don't think God cares at all how frustrated and overworked I am!"

Next morning in my "devotions" I would beg His forgiveness for all my resentment against Him (never really sure He would be willing to forgive me for the same sin over and over again).

And then I would dive into another day, never quite satisfied unless I was planning some new program to add to an already over-burdened calendar. Some new program designed by me, energized by me, sparked by me, worked by me, organized by me, handed to the people by me, and (hopefully) "blessed" by the Lord.

The people would "get involved" with these programs, serve on committees, address invitations, keep busy with "busy work" – and feel very good because they were helping to build the church.

"What our church really needs," they would say, "is for more people to 'get involved' *like we are*." There was always a certain amount of spiritual pride underscored by expressions of frustration that more people were not "getting involved."

So, in order for more people to "get involved" I would devise another new program and recruit them to man it. But when the period of "involvement" was over, the spiritual growth it had produced was so infinitesimal as to be unnoticeable.

I found myself measuring individual spiritual growth by some of the same outward standards I had deplored in the established churches:

- how they were picking up the "language"
- whether or not they would pray in public
- regularity of attendance
- how many of the church's activities they involved themselves in
- availability to the organization
- agreement with the pastor!

All the marks of a *truly "involved" churchman.*

I prayed for a "New Testament Church." But I was the biggest roadblock to its development, because I still saw the church as an organization to be built and run and Christianity as receiving Christ and then "getting involved" in the organization. After all, I was sure every program I planned was synonymous with "the work of the Lord." So, to be involved in the program was to be involved in Christian service. And to be involved in the institution was to be involved in Christ.

When we sought answers for the spiritual growth-plateau we had reached, beyond which we seemed unable to progress, the things we found to do were always just more of the same. New programs, new slogans, new personnel — but the same old tired "let's get 'em involved" technique, a technique that all too often backfired as it fostered judgmental and pharisaical attitudes.

We saw signs of all this for a long time but didn't see it nearly so clearly until that "cold" night in September when the bottom fell out at a business meeting. That night the veil over our true level of spiritual maturity was dramatically torn away, showing the raw carnality and spiritual infancy hidden beneath a facade of numerical success and shallow faith.

For six weeks after that crisis, I was in a kind of shock.

The "New Testament Church" I'd been praying for wasn't anywhere in sight.

And I was tired. Tired of struggling. Tired of tension, overwork and frustration. Tired of trying to fulfill the Great Commission *all by myself!* Tired of working so hard to build a church that would be new, different, with a First Century kind of fellowship — only to discover that some of the old dreaded institutional diseases were infecting our "new" church.

I loved God. I knew I was called to preach. At other times when things went wrong in my ministry, I had talked of forsaking my ordination to become a layman, but my conscience told me such a decision would be impossible to live with. During *this* period of re-evaluating my place in God's plan, I did not seriously consider leaving the ministry. I thought, instead, that I would get a secular job and try to get people involved in home Bible study groups and give up forever the idea of trying to build an "institution."

"New Testament life can't happen within the organized church," I concluded. "There is too much against it!"

Too many "barnacles" from the past still cling to the old institutional church concept.

Too much emphasis on buildings and budgets. Too much money needed just to keep the machine running. Too much pastoral and lay effort spent on oiling the gears of the organization. Too much energy expended keeping touchy members happy because you can't afford to lose them.

Too much dependence on the pastor — and no way to change that.

Too many comfortable pews all facing the front so no one has to relate to anyone else. Too easy for Christians to sit-listen-leave-and-forget without anything really happening in their lives.

Too much holding one another at arm's length. Too little real fellowship — gut-level fellowship — inner circle fellowship. Nothing provided in the church to make it happen at that level.

Too many rules. Too much government. Too many man-made standards. Too many reports to fill out.

Too little time to enjoy life.

Too little time with the family.

Too little time to get to know God. Too little time to pray.

There seems to be no way for people to get free from the notion that Christianity is activity in an organization that owns a building someplace. There is no thought of finding one's own ministry under the personal leadership of the Holy Spirit. Christians never get that free from "the Church."

I could see these things, but I did not know how else to operate. All my ministerial training in college had taught me how to function within this old mold. All my experience had been in making the old outdated machine run at top efficiency when in reality the old machine was almost ready for the junkpile. A new day demanded a new vehicle for moving the Great Commission forward.

I became convinced that the organized church as I knew it — even *my own* new church — would never be that vehicle. There was too much against it.

There was just *no way*.

I deeply longed to lead my young congregation into the experience of the Church in *Acts*. But I'd tried every idea my cleverness could devise to lead it to such a life — but no program of mine could bring it off.

I'd have been willing to listen to any advice that made any kind of sense and provided answers to any of the questions I was asking. But, *who* do you go to for advice when you are convinced that no other pastor you know is any freer from the institutional hang-ups than you are, and no church you know is any closer to the New Testament Ideal than the one you serve?

Others were asking the same questions I was, and were decrying the same institutional sins — but no one's "answers" ever seemed to get below the surface. They never seemed to be suggesting anything but another form of programming and human manipulation to try to make the old dead body *appear* to be new and alive.

Or, at the other extreme, while trying to get rid of the old, out-worn peripheral junk that *needs* to be scrapped, they were discarding many of the *absolutely vital things* without which true Christianity cannot survive and without which it is quite dead.

Who do you go to for help in leading baby Christians to spiritual maturity when you feel that those to whom you go for help have been no more successful than you in doing it – or when you believe that what they consider to be the marks of the mature Christian are actually only phony add-ons "worn" by baby Christians to make them *appear* mature?

So there I stood, my illusions lying in a crumbling heap around me. The stark reality of our spiritual stagnation stared me in the face. There was nowhere to look for answers. There were none within me. I was unable to unlock the ones hidden in the Bible. There were none available in my contemporaries. I was frustrated. Alone. Discouraged. Too hung up in the institutional concept *myself* ever to see the way out.

So . . . . why *not* just leave it all behind?

Rediscovery of New Testament life for the church can never take place as long as men who make up the church are satisfied with the status quo or cling to the conviction that *they* are capable of solving its problems and renewing it through their own efforts and ingenuity.

The church in Century One was new and alive and powerful and miraculous, not because it had more clever members than we do, or better-trained leaders, or less to distract it from its commitment – but because everything it had was given it by God and everything it was was produced by Christ in it and everything it did was done through it by the Holy Spirit. It saw itself as nothing and having nothing apart from Jesus Christ.

Men, made out of the same mud as I am, stood alone, afraid. An impossible commission had been dumped into their reluctant laps. They stood as weak and powerless and helpless to make

Acts happen among them as I was to make it happen in the twentieth century.

They were at the place where they could do *nothing* . . . except either *wait* or *run.*

Then at precisely the right moment, God moved into their seeming impasse. And, they began to live new lives on a new level and to experience a life together that gave them such a sense of belonging that they were even willing to die together for the Lord Jesus.

Their *mission impossible* became *mission accomplished.*

The place where I have no more solutions, and no one else to whom to turn, is the place where renewal can begin. Until then, I am the biggest roadblock in its way.

III

RENEWAL BEGINS WITH "NUMBER ONE"

God's timing is always perfect. He's never late. And He knows exactly the strategic moment to move.

(If only I could remember it whenever a crisis hits!)

In two weeks (the fifth and sixth weeks of my "period of shock"), the spirit brought three men across my path. And what He said to me through these three men is completely changing my ministry . . . and me.

A Watchman and "The Body"

Into the darkness of bewilderment that surrounded me during those forty-five days of groping, walked a lady member of my church — a lady I had considered as one of my "weaker members."

I was a little irritated as I answered the doorbell on my "day off" and was confronted by this lady, who was saying something like, "I've just finished reading this book, Pastor Bob. And I received such a lot of help from it, I thought you would like to read it."

I took the little green book, smiling a phony smile, and mumbling something about how *glad* I would be to read it (inwardly wondering why people were always bringing things to me to read, when I barely had time to read my Bible and my newspaper — especially on my day off!)

Later that day, I did begin to read the little green book. I soon was so involved in it I couldn't lay it down. The writer was saying exactly the things I needed to hear at that decisive time in my ministry.

The book was authored by a Chinese Christian with the strange name of Watchman – Watchman Nee. It bore the title, *What Shall This Man Do?* [1]

I discovered that Watchman Nee has a special gift of insight into the Scriptures that is rare. He sees it not as a book of proof-texts for his doctrinal positions, but as the revelation of the Person and work of God through His Son, Jesus Christ.

I found myself confronting spiritual reality as I had seldom done before. To this Chinese preacher, every word of Scripture is true and not subject to doubt. Jesus Christ is alive – genuinely, personally, *really* alive! And Watchman Nee never thinks of Him any other way.

I often entertained doubts. I doubted, at times, the reality of the resurrection, the reality of my new birth, and even in really "low" times, the existence of God. Of course, I never expressed these doubts to anyone, but they were there sometimes and they were real. I would muster all my carefully learned theological arguments to work through these doubts logically. These arguments were always sufficient to "bring me back." But, I often wondered why a Christian minister should have such doubts at all.

To this man, Nee, everything about Jesus Christ and life in the Spirit was undeniable reality. Experiential reality.

Then . . . he began to talk about the church:

> God is not satisfied with single, separate Christians. When we believed on the Lord and partook of Him, we became members of His Body. Oh, that God would cause this fact to break upon us! Do I seek spiritual experiences for myself? Do I make converts for my denomination? Or have I caught the wisdom of the one heavenly Man, [2] and realized that God is seeking to bring men into that? When I do, salvation, deliverance, enduement with the Spirit, yes, everything in Christian experience will be seen from a new viewpoint; everything for me will be transformed. [3]

[1] Published by Christian Literature Crusade, Fort Washington, Pennsylvania, 1967, for the U.S.A. market, and by Victory Press, Lottbridge Drove, Eastbourne, Sussex, England, for all sales outside the U.S.A. Used by permission.

[2] The Church, in Ephesians 2:15.

[3] Watchman Nee, "*What Shall This Man Do?*", page 74.

I found my heart praying the prayer his book includes:

> As we go further with these studies, I hope some of the vastness of God's purpose in the church will become apparent to us. But that is not enough. My prayer, my longing, is that we may see Christ in fullness. It is not sufficient that we seek hereafter to build up, according to Scriptural doctrines, a good, earnest church as men reckon it. No, *light* is our cry. We dare to face the light. "Lord, give me, like Stephen, to see the Son of man in heaven and in His light to see what Thy Church is; Thy work is. And then, grant me grace not only to live and walk, but also to work, in that light!"
>
> The outstanding feature of God's work is not a doctrine but a life, and life comes by revelation in the light of God. Behind doctrine there may be nothing but words. Behind revelation is God Himself. [4]

I was nearly desperate to "see what Thy Church is," what "Thy work is." So much of what I had seen of the church had too little in it that was clearly "the work of God." I felt that, after fifteen years in the ministry, I still had not "seen" God's Church.

As I read on in this book which to me was the most unusual book I'd ever read outside the Bible; I began to see that *most of my work* as a minister had been *my own* and not His. Wood, hay and stubble! [5] It could all be so easily explained. It was all so human, so much a thing of my own effort and carefully calculated to bring maximum glory to *me*.

> Not merely what we preach, but what we are, weighs with God, not doctrine; but the character of Christ wrought out in us by God's orderings, by God's testings, but the Spirit's patient workings. Work that is of God is work that has been to the Cross. When our work has been that way, we can rest assured that it will in the end survive the fire. Not, "Where is the need most evident? What ideas and resources have *I* got? How much can *I* do? How soon can *I* put that doctrine into practice?" But, "Where is God moving? What is there of *Him* here? How far is it *His* will for me to go?

[4] Ibid., page 85.
[5] 1 Corinthians 3:12-15.

What is the mind of the *Spirit* on this?" – These are the questions of the truly crucified servant.[6]

* * *

Wood, Hay, Stubble; these suggest what is essentially of man and of the flesh. They imply what is common, ordinary, easily and cheaply acquired – and of course perishable.[7]

* * *

All flesh, all mere feelings, all that is essentially of man, is grass and must vanish away. What is of Christ, the gold, the silver, the costly stones; these alone are eternal, incorruptible, imperishable.[8]

* * *

As a man's personality is expressed through his body, so is Christ displayed through the Church. She is in this age the vessel which, in a spiritual sense, contains and reveals Christ.[9]

* * *

Ask yourself, "The work I have done, that for which I have lived and poured out my strength, what is it?" . . . When, in the light of His Word, we see God's purpose in His Son, everything is transformed. We still preach, but we see differently. Nothing we do thereafter stands alone. All is for one thing – the eternal self-revelation of Christ through His Body.[10]

* * *

To create an earthly thing is easy for us. If we are content with an outward, technical Christianity – a "movement" based on an earthly foundation, with an earthly structure and organization – then it is quite possible to do the thing ourselves. But we have been apprehended for something utterly different from this. The Church is spiritual, and her work is heavenly. It must never become earth-bound.[11]

* * *

The work of Christ now is to love and cherish her, to protect and preserve her from disease and blemish; caring thus for her because He loves her as His own self – because, speaking reverently, the Church is Christ![12]

[6] Nee, "*What Shall This Man Do?*", page 87.
[7] Ibid., page 88.
[8] Ibid., page 89.
[9] Ibid., page 91.
[10] Ibid., page 91.
[11] Ibid., page 92.
[12] Ibid., page 97.

That statement sent me rushing for my Bible. Could Christ *really* be that completely identified with His church?

Sure enough — in Ephesians 5:30, Paul says, "We are members of his body, *of his flesh and his bones.*"

And in First Corinthians 6:15, believers are called *"the members of Christ."*

And in Acts 9:5 . . . But that's where Watchman Nee himself begins in Chapter 7 of his book . . . (The marginal headings are mine.)

> From the heavenly mystery, we turn now to the earthly expression. Having seen the Church, the Body, in her relation to her Lord, we must now consider her relationships. The time has come to ask ourselves, "How do the members function one towards another?"
>
> *Christ and His Disciples Are One*
>
> It seems likely that, of all the apostles, it was to Paul first that there came the concept of Jesus and His people as a body and its members. Certainly, it is a view of the Church that is peculiarly his. It was, after all, bound up with his very conversion and calling, being contained in the Lord's first words to him: "I am Jesus whom thou persecutest" (Acts 9:5). To persecute those who believe is to persecute Jesus. To touch His disciples is to touch Him. Thus, these words heralded the great revelation that was to be given to Paul of the mystery of the Church. They told him something new about the Lord, something till then no more than implicit in His statements while on earth.
>
> *Individualism Is Sin*
>
> But the Lord did not leave the matter there with Paul. He did not allow him to stay with the heavenly mystery. The command that immediately followed came right down to the practical consequences of such a revelation. "Rise, and enter into the city, and it shall be told thee what thou must do." *It shall be told thee.* Apart from those very disciples against whom he had set himself, Paul would be helpless; he would never know. The Lord Himself would not tell him what to do, save on the basis of the living Church. He would not lend His support to a merely individual calling and mission. For individualism is sin; it does injury to the Body of Christ.
>
> So Paul reached Damascus, and there followed for him long hours of waiting. At first no man came. Only after three days of darkness did someone at length arrive — and

even then, he was but "a disciple." From Luke's use of this simple title, we are to conclude that Ananias, though devout and of honorable character, was just an ordinary brother, with nothing special about him to qualify him as the helper of the destined "great apostle of the Church." But, it is just here that the mystery of the Church must become practical for Paul.[13]

* * *

The Church As Christ Incarnate

God's principle is the principle of incarnation. (We use the term with caution. It is unwise to carry too far the parallel between the Church and her incarnate Lord.) God desires—indeed for Him it is more than a desire; it is a divine necessity — to show the heavenly life in an earthly expression, not in angels or spirits but in men; not as something vague and imaginery, but in a form that is real and practical . . . God's character demands that His Church, universal, spiritual, heavenly, should have its earthly expression in local churches, set in places no less dark than the pagan city of Corinth . . . I Corinthians 12 shows us that even in such an earthly environment, the church is to operate on the principles of the heavenly Body. For the local church is not merely an outward type, it is a real manifestation of Christ in the earth today. "Ye are the Body of Christ." Here in Corinth, you Corinthian believers are called to be the whole Body in essence.

Taking Responsibility

So we turn to I Corinthians 12 and its treatment of the functional life of the Body. If we look closely at the section of this chapter from verse 12 onwards, I think we can discern four simple laws governing the Body's life.

You Must Function As You Are

The first is in verses 15 and 16: "If the foot shall say, Because I am not the hand, I am not of the body; it is not, therefore, not of the body. And, if the ear shall say, Because I am not the eye, I am not of the body; it is not, therefore, not of the body." In other words, you must function as you are, and not as you would prefer to be. Because you are not someone else, that is no ground for declining to be yourself! It is as though the foot said, "I had made up my mind to be a hand, and because I can't, I'll refuse to walk!" Such refusal springs from a comparing heart, and only individualism compares.

[13] Ibid., pages 99-100.

Every Member Is Needed

This habit of making comparisons reveals one thing, that we have not yet seen the Body of Christ. For tell me, which is the better member, the foot or the hand? There is, when you come to think of it, no way of comparing them. Their function in the human body is different, and each is equally needed there. And yet, many, thus, minimize God's gift. Because they cannot be the special member they admire, thy decline to take their place at all. Or they think all ministry begins and ends with public ministry; and because they have not the gift to function in a public way, they do nothing.[14]

* * *

How the Church Discovers Life

It is by functioning that we discover life. The Church is suffering not as much from the prominence of the five-talent members as from the holding back of the one-talent members.[15] The life of the whole Body is hampered and impoverished by the burial of those single talents.

If we have once recognized the heavenly Body, we shall be very glad to have the tiniest part in it. Of course, refusal to function because we have only one talent may reveal in us desires and ambitions outside the will of God, or worse, a dissatisfaction with that will. But no, if it pleases Him to make me the greatest member, praise the Lord! If He chooses instead to make me the least, praise Him no less! [16]

* * *

Paul wrote: "Encourage the faint-hearted" (I Thessalonians 5:14), and the word is literally "small-souled." We should encourage the one-talent man, not because of the magnitude of his gift — it isn't so very big after all — but because the Holy Spirit indwells him. His ground of expectation is to be God Himself. One of my own closest colleagues, before he was born again, was regarded by his friends as incredibly dull, indeed almost stupid. Yet, when God took hold of his life and the Holy Spirit began to work in him, within two years he already showed signs of becoming, as he now is, one of the most gifted Bible teachers in China.

The First Law of Function

So the first law of function is that we use what we have been given. We cannot excuse ourselves and say, "I am not needed here." Nor shall we find spiritual refreshment by taking our Bibles and notebooks and retiring to a quiet spot to prepare for some imagined future ministry, if in so doing,

[14] Ibid., pages 102-103.
[15] Matthew 25:14-30.
[16] Nee, *"What Shall This Man Do?"*, pages 103-104.

we are evading a present responsibility . . . the rule is always to serve others with what we have in hand, and as we do so, to discover that we ourselves are fed.[17]

* * *

Two-Way Fellowship

The fellowship of the Body is always two-way: receiving and giving. Wanting only to receive is not fellowship. We may not be preachers, but when we come to worship we nevertheless bring what we have. There must be help to the pulpit from the pew. Sitting and looking on will not do. We must give others to drink, not necessarily by speaking, but maybe by quiet prayer. And if we do just sit and listen, we must be there in spirit, not somewhere else! [18]

* * *

Every Member Has a Ministry

So every member of the Body has a ministry, and every member is called to function in the place appointed by the Lord. It makes no difference who does the work if the glory is His. We must turn to God's account the position given us by Him and not run off hoping to grow in retirement.

Accepting Limitation

The Second Law of Function

The second law of function is found in verses 17 and 18: "If the whole body were an eye, where were the hearing? If the whole were hearing, where were the smelling? But now hath God set the members each one of them in the body, even as it pleased him." The principle here set forth is that in our life together, we are always to leave room for the function of others.

Give Others a Chance to Function

Putting it bluntly, do not try to do everything and be everything yourself! No one in his senses would desire to see the whole Body function merely in a single way. It is not reasonable for the whole to be an eye, nor for the eye to attempt the work of the whole. The Lord has ordered variety in the Body, an ear and a nose as well as an eye and a hand; not conformity, and certainly not single-organ monoply. Thus, if the previous principle was for those lagging behind, this one is for those who are too forward, wanting to be the whole Body. The word to them is, I repeat, don't try to do or be everything; you are *not* everything! [19]

* * *

[17] Ibid., page 104.
[18] Ibid., pages 104-105.
[19] Ibid., pages 105-106.

One Cause of Frustration

There is much frustration and loss among the members of Christ today because some of us who are experienced servants of God are not willing to let others function. We have been given a ministry by the Lord, and for this reason we think we must bear the whole responsibility ourselves if others are to develop and grow. We have not understood that by doing so we are in fact hindering the development of those others. This mistake is a fruitful source of discouragement and even division, and its ill effects do not end there.[20]

* * *

How Doctrinal Differences Start

For let us suppose that I encounter a doctrinal point of which I cannot see the answer and find myself in a fog about it. What do I do? Do I try to decide it myself, or do I go to the member whose special gift from God is the capacity to teach and clarify and to lead people out of doctrinal fogs? If I do the former, I have opened the way for a new doctrinal difference, for it is at this very point that doctrinal differences have their birth. Instead of trusting the Lord to solve my problem through His teaching member and so letting another member function for me in this matter, I have made it all too possible for the two of us to be found teaching different and even conflicting things."[21]

* * *

I Must Be Willing to Be Ministered To

As a member, I must be prepared to receive what another member has to give. For myself, I must be willing for limitation. Is the church at prayer? I must be ready to remain silent and to give room for the "weaker" prayers. Have I a gift of preaching? I must learn to sit and listen to others. Be my measure small or large, I dare not, as a member, go beyond it, for the mark of the Cross is upon all that is oversize; all that is extraneous to the Body. I must be willing to be limited entirely to my sphere and to let others serve in theirs. I must be happy for others to function towards me and to accept the help ministered to me by them.

Esteeming Others

Thirdly, we come to verses 21 and 22: "The eye cannot say to the hand, I have no need of thee; or again, the head to the feet, I have no need of you. Nay, much rather, those members of the Body which seem to be more feeble are necessary." Put quite simply, we must never seek to cut off

[20] Ibid., page 106.
[21] Ibid., pages 106-107.

Weaker Members Are Necessary

another member. We must not think we can act in the capacity of the Head and dispense with the members. Weakness or uncouthness in a member is no warrant for our cutting him off. We dare not say to another: "I have no need of thee." Rather do we discover how much we can learn from members we would not naturally esteem. We may often have to call for prayer-help from those we might even be inclined to despise. Alas, how readily do we feel we should demean ourselves and lose our spiritual status by so doing! Yet, the Lord affirms that He has a place for, and can use, even the feeblest of His members.[22]

That hit too hard! And it checked out with everything the Bible teaches. But there were a lot of people in both my past and my present I felt *sure* I would be better off without. I felt I could get along quite nicely if they would just move far, far away. But now I reluctantly began to see that they were in the church, in all their uncouthness and weakness, to minister to the Body – and to *me!* I accepted it, because I was trying so hard to "find the Church." But it would be easier to accept the *concept* than the "weaker members" themselves.

I read Watchman Nee with an open Bible and an open mind, opened by the frustration I felt about the church as I was experiencing it. As I read his book and dug into the Word to see if these things were so, [23] I began to get a glimpse of God's plan for the true spiritual Church.

It began to soak in that every individual Christian is a minister and a priest, [24] whose spiritual ministry is deeply needed in the church. That the church is as sick as it is to a large degree because every individual Christian does not see himself as a minister and priest, nor is there any real encouragement for him to see himself that way. The spiritual ministry of each individual member must be a *spiritual* ministry – not just more involvement in the machinery of an organization.

Hesitantly, a little fearfully, I began to get the picture that, in God's program for the Body, they, *as much if not more than I,* have spiritual life and strength to minister to the church and each

[22] Ibid., page 107.
[23] Acts 17:11.
[24] 1 Peter 2:5, 9.

other – the kind of spiritual ministry that simply is *not* being utilized in the church today, because *no opportunity is provided* for its utilization.

Keeping the Unity

There Must Be No Division

And . . . verses 24 and 25 tell us: "God tempered the body together, giving more abundant honor to that part which lacked; that there should be no schism in the body; but that the members should have the same care one for another." What the apostle here says in conclusion is that we are resolutely to refuse schism. It is totally disallowed. The divine will is that *there should be no schism in the Body*. . . . The Church, as seen in heaven, cannot be divided. Praise God, it is one forever. Yes, but there can be inroads upon that unity in the church on earth. As to its heavenly life, the Body is untouchable; but in its functioning on earth it is all too sadly true that it can be touched and even mutilated, as the Corinthian situation abundantly shows. Paul condemns this state of affairs in no uncertain terms.

* * *

What Makes the Body One

What then, is the secret of practical units? Here are two statements about it. "For in one Spirit were we all baptized into one body, whether Jews or Greeks, whether bond or free; and were all made to drink of one Spirit" (I Cor. 12:13). "There is one body and one Spirit" (Eph. 4:4). What they reveal is a remarkable relation between the Body and the Spirit. The hidden reality, the Spirit, has its counterpart in the manifestation, the Body. The Body is one because the Spirit is one. For remember, the Holy Spirit is a Person, and you cannot subdivide a person. "God tempered the body together," because the one Body is to be a manifestation of the one Spirit. There is always unity in the Spirit. The divine fact is certain. The only question is, do we always give diligence to keep the unity? (Eph. 4:3).

* * *

Unity Starts With "The Life"

Before proceeding to a further word about the Holy Spirit and the Body, let us remind ourselves that the starting-point for spiritual unity is life. You may already have observed that the four principles we have outlined above are not in fact expressed as commands at all. They appear in I Corinthians 12 in the form of statements of what the Body is *like*. They describe it in terms of the spontaneous manifestations of life and growth in a human body. This is significant, and it brings us to consider an important feature of life; namely, consciousness.

Consciousness of Life

All animal life has consciousness, but especially is this true of life from God. Where there is life there is consciousness. A biologist has no way of taking up life as a separate thing and handing it to us to touch or look at, nor is there any way by which we could see it if he did. Yet all will agree that, because of our inward consciousness, we know we have life. We are in no doubt at all that we live. And the same is true of the new life. Though the life that God gives cannot be handled or seen, it is certainly possible for us to be conscious of it. We know new life because with it there is awakened in us a new consciousness. When a man is born again, he receives new life from God. How does he *know* he has received it? How do any of us know we possess new life? We know by a new life consciousness. If the life is there, the consciousness will be there and will very soon manifest itself towards God and towards sin. If we sin there is distress. We lose something of our peace and joy. It is this that proves the presence of life. Because the life of God hates sin, there has come to be in us a new consciousness towards sin. When a man constantly needs someone to point out his sins to him and is otherwise unaware of them himself, then, however willing to listen he may be, it is more than doubtful whether he possesses life. Today we place great emphasis on life, but that is not enough. We should emphasize also the consciousness of life. A being without consciousness has very little evidence of life. For it is a misunderstanding to think of life as abstract. It is concrete; real. In a human heart, either new life is present or it is absent; and life-consciousness is what confirms its presence. Nor is this consciousness merely negative towards sin. It is also blessedly positive towards God Himself. The Spirit witnesses with our spirit that we are the children of God – yes, but it is no use telling people that! Either they know it, or they don't. If they possess God's life, they know it by the Spirit.

* * *

Consciousness of the Life of the Body

But if what we have said is true of the life of the individual, it is no less true of the life of the Body. Those who possess life possess it in common with others, and they who know the Body are conscious of the corporate character of that life. For the Body is not only a principle or a doctrine; it, too, implies a consciousness. As we are conscious of new life, so, if we are within the Body, we must necessarily be conscious also of that.

Some act towards the Body much as people do who determine to love their enemies because it is a Christian duty, or not to tell lies because it is wrong. But while it is very important whether we lie or not, what is far more important is whether, if we do we are troubled inside. Inner consciousness of God and inner sensitiveness to sin are the basis of Christianity, these and not outward rules. So it is little use trying to live by the principle of the Body unless we are conscious that something is wrong when we do not. It is one thing to be told, and quite another to see. Consciousness is that inner sense that sees without being told. If the entrance of divine light can give in our hearts the consciousness of God and of sin that is against God, it can give a like consciousness of the Body and of conduct that is against Christ as Head of the Body. It was light from God that awakened in Paul a consciousness of the Body and showed him that he was opposing himself to Jesus in the person of His members. Without the consciousness that comes from revelation and life, all is empty indeed.

"Love One Another"

How to Know You Are Alive

Let me try now to illustrate the working of this factor that I have called "Body-Consciousness" — this sensitiveness to the Body of Christ. It works first of all in the matter of love. "We know that we have passed out of death into life, because we love the brethren" (I John 3:14). All who are members of the Body, love. This is remarkable. It is not that any need to wait till they are told. Spontaneously, whether they think about it or not, they love. They may need exhortation, but that is in order to stir up what they have. I remember a friend telling me how, when his first child was put into his arms, his heart went out in love to him. No one needed to tell him it was a father's duty to love his child. He simple found love there. But, is it not equally true that, no matter who or what a brother is, as soon as you know he is a Christian, your heart goes out in love to him? This is consciousness of the Body.

Division Is a Foreign World

It works also in regard to division. Whereas in respect of love it is active and positive, in respect of division it is passive and negative. To those who have truly discovered the meaning of the Body, all division, and everything that makes for division is hateful in the extreme. To be found

> differentiating between Christians is, for them, to have stepped into a foreign world. Whether it is right or not to glory in denominationalism, those who recognize the Body of Christ know that to do so is an impossibility. A sectarian spirit, however hallowed by tradition and use, soon becomes intolerable to the man who possesses life.[25]

Such thoughts as these cut squarely across many of my own motives for building the church. Again, I checked Mr. Nee against the Scriptures, determined now to accept what they said, even if what they said seemed unworkable or condemned some of the things I was doing and my motives for doing them. I wanted more than ever to "see God's Church." No matter how many new questions and problems it would raise.

> If the Body means anything to us, all that divides within and without becomes abhorrent. Even to begin to create division is to forfeit our inward peace. We know we cannot go on. The consciousness of the one life will not allow it, and that is the sufficient answer.
>
> This is not doctrine, but the living consciousness of our fellowship in Christ; and it is a very precious thing. The instant life comes to us, it awakens in us a growing and deepening sense of "belonging." We can no longer live a self-interested, self-sufficient Christian life. The nature of the butterfly, always "going it alone," has given place in us to the nature of the bee, always operating from the hive, always working not for itself, but for the whole. Body-consciousness means that we see our own standing before God, not as isolated units but as members one of another.
>
> Units have no special use, exercise no ministry, can easily be overlooked or left out. Whether they are present or not is no one's concern. They scarcely affect even statistics. But members are otherwise. They cannot be passive in the Body; they dare not merely stand by looking on. For none are so hurtful as onlookers. Whether or not we take a public part in things is immaterial; we must always be giving life, so that our absence is felt. We cannot say "I don't count." We dare not attend meetings merely as passengers, while others do the work. We are His Body and members in particular, and it is when all the members fulfill their ministry that the life flows.

[25] Nee, *"What Shall This Man Do?"*, pages 109-112.

The Life of the Body Is Everything

For all is bound up with life and the source of life. The head is the life-source of the human body; injure it and all movement, all coordination ceases. A headless torso has neither life nor consciousness of life. As members of Christ, we receive new life from Him; but that life is "in the Son," it is not something that we can carry away with us apart from Him. Detach us for one moment from Christ, and we should have no life. We well know how even a shadow between ourselves and Him may stem for a while its flow. For our life is *in Him;* we possess nothing in ourselves. They have the life who have the Son.

God does not, therefore, tell us to hold fast our fellow-members, but to "hold fast the Head." This is the way of fellowship. For Christ is not divided; He is one. Lay hold of Him, and we shall find welling up in our heart a spontaneous love for all who do the same.

Marks of a Phony Fellowship

Oneness is Christ's, not ours. Because we are His, *therefore* we are one. For example, to say we have fellowship with a brother because we like him is to violate the oneness by centering it in ourselves. Though we may not naturally take to some so readily as others, to let this affect our fellowship is simply to reveal its false basis. Or again, do we do something for a brother and then complain of his ingratitude? That can only be because we did it seeking thanks, and not for Christ's sake — not because, in the first place, God so loved us. Our motive was wrong, because our relation to the Head was deficient.

No Room for Exclusive Friendships

It is "holding fast" to our fellow members that leads to exclusive friendships. The Body has no room for these. If one Christian becomes infatuated with another so that an unhealthy friendship develops, sure enough, before long their friendship will issue in faction. For fellowship that is "after the flesh" is on a wrong foundation and can only lead eventually to sorrow. When two members cling exclusively to one another, we may justifiably fear that the love they express is not purely of God. "Love one another" is either something in the sphere of the Body, and therefore Christ-centered, or it is wrong. May God save us from uncrucified natural choices, and help us in these things to follow the Spirit.[26]

* * *

[26] Ibid., pages 113-114.

"Hold Fast the Head"

Saul's life of fellowship began when he said, "What shall I do, Lord?" This is the secret. To "hold fast the Head" is to *obey* Christ through the Spirit. To follow the Spirit is to be subject to the Lord Jesus in all things. The Spirit will never impose that obedience on the members, but they who live by the anointing will always, instinctively and gladly, subject themselves to Christ; and in doing so, they will discover their oneness. Oh, to see Him, then, as unquestioned Lord! [27]

Here was Christ operating as the Head of His Church. It began to dawn on me that I had never allowed Christ to be Head of His own Body! I had been its head. In every church I'd ever seen in operation, even though we often spoke of Him as Head, in reality, it was a pastor or a board or a congregational meeting that ran the church. Not on the basis of a powerful sensed unity in the Spirit, but on the basis of majority rule. All the decisions were made by men. All the strategies, programs and organizations were arranged by human ingenuity; and then "sanctified" by a quick glib prayer asking the Lord to "bless these plans, this program, this organization."

"But He expects to do it through us." Perhaps. But . . . *He* expects to do it.

I had little idea how Christ could actually and practically be allowed to direct church affairs as more than just a titular head. But I now saw that *somehow, somewhere* we had to begin to find out how.

As I considered these things (often with a lump in my throat as the excitement of these "new" discoveries would grip me), I saw my long-cherished role in the church dwindling to its Scriptural size before my eyes — eyes that were "seeing the church" for the first time. The pastor, in the New Testament Church, is *not everything*. He is just one of Christ's gifts to the church. [28] And, in the local expression of Christ's Body, he is by no means the only one with something to share. In fact, *every* believer has a gift (or gifts), [29] *every* believer has a ministry, [30] *every* believer

[27] Ibid., pages 115-116
[28] Ephesians 4:11.
[29] 1 Corinthians 12:7-12.
[30] Ephesians 4:12.

is a priest,[31] *every* believer has something to offer to every meeting of the Body.[32] The Church was never meant to be a one-man show. The Body was never expected to draw all its life, teaching and leadership from any one person – however spiritual or well-trained that person might be.[33]

I was aware of a new sensation of hope working its way into my emotions – new hope for my church. It came as I began to see that every one of my church people, no matter how young and immature in the Lord he might be, possesses the Life of Jesus Christ in Him. In the New Testament Church, they counted on that. I didn't. But, I was willing to begin – if I could just figure out how.

I had read the things about which Watchman Nee spoke dozens of times in the Bible – without ever "seeing" them. But the Holy Spirit brought me to them at a crucial time in my ministry – through the gifts of this imprisoned Chinese Christian.

I now saw God's work in the light of New Testament revelation. I now saw the life the Body was to share. I now saw the view it was to have of itself. I realized the importance of each member discovering his personal ministry and being allowed to minister to all the other members.

But how? What kind of church structure will it take to produce such a mutual ministry? Present structures certainly are wrong for it.

And what kind of a man could lead the church in such a direction? How would the church respond to such leadership? Could *I* ever shake free enough from the machine and my own inner struggles to do it?

[31] 1 Peter 2:5, 9.
[32] 1 Corinthians 14:26.
[33] Ephesians 4:16.

IV

RENEWAL BEGINS WITH "NUMBER ONE" (Continued)

A Major and "The Life"

As I look back on it, I can only conclude that God's timing and dealing with me at this time were miraculous.

While I was reading the Nee book, Carl and I attended the monthly meeting of the Phoenix Association of Evangelical Ministers. The speaker's name meant nothing to us, and we had no idea what his subject would be.

A gray-haired Englishman with a little mustache, a characteristic little cough, and a beautiful accent was introduced as Major W. Ian Thomas [1] of Capernwray Fellowship of Torchbearers, a retired officer of the Royal Fusiliers.

He began talking about people who were *tired.* I identified with every sentence. I was dreadfully tired.

He spoke of Christians who had no peace, no rest, in spite of the fact that Christ had promised both. I was the Christian about whom he was speaking. I couldn't remember the last time I had felt really at peace. I was driven by all the condemning guilts and self-made laws that he said drive people.

He spoke of being "fit to quit."

"That's me!" I whispered to Carl.

"Me, too!" he nodded.

"Jesus said, 'Come unto me, all ye that labor and are heavy laden, and *I will give you rest.*'" The Major was reading Matthew 11:28.

[1] Major Thomas' special emphasis can also be seen in the reading of his book *The Saving Life of Christ,* published by Zondervan.

"Rest? What's that?" I said to myself almost bitterly, "I don't know what it is to stop struggling, clawing, fighting, straining – pushing hard against time and circumstances and a heavy work load. I really don't have the foggiest idea what Jesus was talking about!"

"If you are digging a hole," the Major went on, "and I come and say to you, 'I'm going to give you a rest,' what do you expect me to do? Sing you a song? Quote Bible verses to you? Give you a new shovel?

"No! You will expect me to climb down into the hole and dig, while you climb out and rest.

"That is what Jesus means to do for you, when He says 'I will give you rest.' He expects you to *quit,* so He can get down into your hole and do the digging!"

As he spoke, referring to several familiar sections of the New Testament, I saw that Jesus Christ was really alive and living in me for the purpose of daily living His life in me and through me. No one had ever told me this before. Or . . . maybe I had never before stopped my mad rush long enough to listen.

"For if, when we were enemies we were reconciled to God by the death of his Son, much more, being reconciled, we shall be saved (daily) by his life" (Romans 5:10).

Saved by His Life.

I realized as this man spoke that I had experienced only the first half of that verse – "reconciled to God by the death of his Son . . ." My sins were forgiven. I was sure that the moment I died, I would be with Jesus, experiencing eternal life. My faith was there.

But I'd never noticed the last half of that verse, even though I'd read it a hundred times.

". . . Much more, being reconciled we shall be saved by his *life.*"

"Quit!" Major Thomas was advising us. Begin to depend upon the Life of Jesus to live the Christian life in and through you. Quit trying to fulfill the Great Commission, obey the commandments, fulfill your ministerial calling. Instead, depend on the Life – *His* Life in you. If He doesn't do it, nobody should.

Simply make your body available to Him. Quit! and let Jesus be in you what the New Testament declares that He is. Don't try to be "like Jesus." Let Jesus live your life. Stop doing things for Him. Start letting Him do it.

Rest! And watch what Jesus Christ alive in you can do.

It made too much sense for me to be able to ignore the message.

I saw Jesus as alive — *really* alive — for the first time since becoming a Christian. I saw Him elevated above doctrine, history, the organized church and even His own Word. I saw Him as solidly relevant to every moment of my life.

I went home that afternoon and sat down behind my desk and followed the man's advice. "Lord," I said aloud, "I'm *tired* and I *quit!* From now on if you want anything done around here, *You* will have to be the one to do it! I am available. You can use me any way and anytime You wish. But from now on I'm not going to move unless You move me.

"I'm quitting as pastor of this church. You be the pastor from now on. If You choose to do it through me, or through someone else, it makes no difference — as long as it's You doing it. You do the preaching, leading and counseling. If You want anyone won to You, You'll have to do it.

"I love You. I'm available. I want to be used, if You can use me. But I can't do this work anymore! It's too much for me. It's Your baby, Lord, from here on out.

"I quit!"

Carl told me later, he did the same thing that day. He was quicker than I was to follow through on a day-to-day basis. He was of great help in showing me how to rest and to let Jesus live His life and do His work through me.

Imperfectly, with many backslidings, I began to learn to trust Him daily — and for the first time in my life as a Christian, I learned to rest, and to walk, live and work in the power of the Spirit, instead of the energy of the flesh.

For the first time, I knew peace.

In a matter of days, I found myself living a brand new life, with new freedom and new faith and new excitement about it all. I felt as though I had been born again, *again!* Jesus was alive . . . in *me*. The doubts were gone. It began to be fun to be alive in Him.

And my ministry and approach to church life began to change.

Programs and clever ideas began to lose their importance. Knowing Christ and helping others to know Him began to be all important.

But how do we translate this into the practical aspects of church life? The institution in its present form will fight these concepts. Its very structure is against this new "faith-rest" principle. How can the people ever catch this for their lives? They're so bound by the organizational concept and its traditions.

Perhaps leaving the institution is *still* the only answer.

A Professor and the Re-formed Church

It nearly never rains in Arizona's desert. But it was raining. I unsuccessfully dodged giant drops as I ran to the mailbox for the day's delivery.

As the rumble of thunder rose and fell and the dark sky pelted my study window with the clatter of droplets, I leafed slowly through the National Association of Evangelicals *Action* magazine.

I stopped turning pages to look more closely into an article titled "Twentieth Century Re-formation." Its author was a Wheaton Graduate School professor named Lawrence O. Richards.[2]

He was telling about an experimental seminar held at Honey Rock Camp Grounds somewhere in the woods of Wisconsin. I wasn't reading at all seriously until certain ideas began to leap off the page at me, yanking me abruptly to attention.

> Our study has led us to describe church forms which would create conditions in which New Testament principles could best operate. We came to believe that for the church to function most effectively in our world

[2] This is now part of a book by Professor Richards titled *A New Face For the Church*, published by Zondervan Publishing House (1970), Grand Rapids, Michigan. The National Association of Evangelicals has also published the articles in their original form in a booklet titled, *Tomorrow's Church Today*.

— the family unit must become the focus of the church's ministry.
— responsibility for nurture and outreach must be shifted from church agencies to believers.
— The church must adopt forms (by forms we mean to include church services, organizations, agencies and ministries) which will support believers in fulfilling their ministries.
— a church which meets these requirements will necessarily face a thorough reorganization; it will be re-formed.

The church itself is extremely simple in structure. I shall first sketch it overall, then look in greater depth at each level.

The family unit is the focal point of ministry. Here, in weekday life, Christian growth primarily takes place. Here too, family members (and the unit) engage in evangelism. Home Bible classes, clearly defined ministries of love and concern to neighboring families as well as personal witness by dad, mom and children, are all means by which others are reached for Christ. Since the re-formed church does not have agencies structured either for nurture or evangelism, responsibility is placed where it belongs — on each believer.

The growth cell is a necessary support for believers-in-families. The small size of the cell and the intimate fellowship developed there gives a context for close support and development of weaker families. The growth cell meets at least once a week, for a sharing Bible study, prayer and discussion.

The congregation is composed of a maximum of 25 growth cells. It meets together once a week on Sunday for a three hour block of time. *No other regular meeting of the congregation is permitted,* although retreats or special study classes of a short-term nature, or special outreach ministries, may be planned.[3]

Concerning the *growth cell,* Professor Richards wrote further:

The growth cell. This structure meets a vital need. Maximum spiritual growth . . . takes place in close fellowship with other believers. Yet in today's church most of our meetings are impersonal. We come to church only to sit and listen. Any conversation with others is usually on a superficial level — "Yes, it is hot." "Did you hear about Brother Brown?" Even in prayer meeting we do not share. We hear the same few pray the same prayers they have prayed for years.

[3] From the article *Twentieth Century Re-formation,"* published in Evangelical Action Magazine, Wheaton, Illinois.

> The growth cell takes on the functions now supposedly fulfilled by the adult Sunday school class and the prayer meeting. In the growth cell God's Word is studied for spiritual growth. Each member shares how God has spoken to him through a common passage. There is no teacher. A growth-by-groups type study guide is used and each individual comes to the cell meeting prepared. Prayer grows out of shared needs as well as requests sent by the pastor to the cell representative. As the fellowship deepens, so does the level of sharing. Soon it is possible truly to "bear one another's burdens" for these are known, and we care.
>
> The growth cell meets in a home for one or two hours a week. The day and hours are selected for the convenience of the members. There are no refreshments. It meets for a spiritual purpose, and this is kept as the sole focus.[4]

His ideas about the growth cells were fresh and new — and, it seemed, also, were *New Testament.* I knew he was talking theory, but it made practical sense in the light of the biblical purposes of the church.

He suggested three prerequisites to effective growth cell life:

(1) The group members must be trained to function in the group.
(2) Each family unit and individual must take responsibility for group life.
(3) The group must be for believers.[5]

The professor's suggestions for the Sunday meeting of *the congregation* were not new — they were *revolutionary!* But my institution-weary heart found them positively delicious.

> The congregational meeting serves several distinct purposes, and the service is designed to attain them. These purposes? (1) To meet the need for a real and sensed unity of the body of Christ gathered. (2) To involve the community in worship, study and planning. (3) To plan for the impact of the church as a whole.
>
> A single three-hour block of time is provided . . . During this time adults and senior highs first gather to hear a message by the pastor. The message is related to the present life and growth of the people. Following the sermon the congregation reacts. Together or in small groups they explore the implications of the Word to individual, family and growth cell life.

[4] Richard's *A New Face For the Church,* pages 32-33.
[5] *Ibid.,* page 34.

> Some Sundays the congregation as a whole will lay plans for their response to the Word taught. On others the period will be used to survey what the children are learning and discuss how the truths can be related to their lives throughout the week. The key concepts, however, are (1) *the sermon is related to developing congregational needs,* and (2) *the people react to each message and discuss its implications for their lives.* The congregational meeting closes with worship.[6]

Richards spoke of the pastor in this re-formed church as "a man who invests his life in the people . . . This man has time to be in the Word and to be with people." [7]

I wanted to be that kind of pastor! ". . . in the Word and . . . with people." In my present approach to ministry both were impossible.

The layman in the re-formed church was described as a man "responsible to be a growing, vital Christian; to contribute to the growth of others in the church and his family; to be a creative witness to Christ in the world." [8] In the re-formed church the layman, not the pastor or some church agency, is charged with the responsibility of soul-winning, and the spiritual development of other Christians. He is to function as what Peter called him in First Peter 2:5 and 9 – a *priest.*

> Luther proclaimed the priesthood of all believers: nearly 500 years later church forms still deny it.[9]

Larry Richards closed his discussion with this sharp challenge:

> You may not like our ideas. If not, we challenge you to improve on them. Most of all, we challenge you to *do something.* If you are not satisfied with the evangelical church today, for Christ's sake, don't just sit there! [10]

I couldn't. I jumped to my feet and shouted to my associate in the office across the hall, "Carl! This is it. This is our answer. I've found our answer!"

[6] *Ibid.,* pages 34-35.
[7] *Ibid.,* page 35.
[8] *Ibid.,* page 38.
[9] *Ibid.,* page 38.
[10] Richards' *Twentieth Century Reformation,* Evangelical *Action* Magazine.

I rushed into Carl's office, magazine in hand, interrupting whatever he was doing.

"Listen to this, man! Here it is."

When I finished reading, we were both so excited we were convinced it had to be right. Maybe we can't use it all. Maybe it will take time to come to some of these things. But something's got to give. We can't just sit — and we can't leave.

"Let's start moving in this direction and see what God will do to Our Heritage!"

We prayed, praised God and began to lay plans that very day to build our whole church program, for families, adults and young people, around *growth cells*. (For a description of the growth-cell life as it evolved at Our Heritage, see Chapters nine and ten).

It would mean a lot of other things would have to go: Midweek service (which we could never get off the ground anyway). Social events. Fisherman's Club. Women's Society. Even Sunday night service. All we had would now be viewed as expendable if it hindered in any way the development of the new style of church life.

I committed myself to a teaching ministry. The evangelistic Sunday morning sermon would fade away to be replaced by messages designed to build disciples. The pastor was going to learn how to be a pastor-teacher instead of an evangelist-program director, public-relations man.

The church would be told that it, not the pastor, was responsible for evangelism. Training would be offered to assist them, but soul-winning in our re-formed church would be viewed as *every* Christian's responsibility.

We would begin experimenting with increasing the effectiveness of the Sunday morning service.

We would gradually phase out all meetings and organizations other than the growth cells and the Sunday congregational meeting. We might not follow the professor's plan for doing business on Sunday morning. It might be necessary to have a monthly business meeting of some kind. But we determined that all business would be cared for either by the church board or the congregation as a whole. No other committees or boards presently in operation would continue longer than necessary to complete business presently before them.

Carl and I were already preaching on the new insights gained from Watchman Nee and Ian Thomas. I would begin immediately to preach on the re-formation needed in the church in the light of New Testament principles I now saw in more vivid perspective than ever. I would seek to show the congregation how the principles presented by Larry Richards could lead to a rediscovery of the life the early Christians shared together.

The ministry of all three of these men came into my life in a two-week period. They came at a time when many of the illusions that might have caused me to resist their ideas had been knocked unceremoniously out of the way, and I saw the immaturity of my church and the ineffectiveness of my own ministry. I was out of gimmicks — and in utter dismay — looking desperately for a way out . . . *or* some real, spiritual *answers.*

These three men presented three phases of the same message — three phases which all telescoped into one thrust toward renewal for our young church. (1) Watchman Nee gave us clear insight into the New Testament concept of the Body, the church, with Christ as its living Head and the Source of all its life. (2) Ian Thomas showed how Life could affect and transform our *personal* Christian lives and ministries. (3) Larry Richards gave us the vehicle for rediscovering the kind of fellowship the church of Century One had, in which Christ can function as Head and His resurrection life can be shared, and in which fellowship gets deeper than the weather and football scores.

And we bought it all. The whole package.

We grabbed these concepts immediately and began to apply them almost at once to our personal lives and then to the life of the church, because they answered all our biggest questions about the church and our ministries in it.

This is not to say all the changes took place overnight. They did not. The readjustment of long-established priorities, the overcoming of deep personal prejudices, fears and hang-ups, the complete metamorphosis in preaching, the learning to depend on *Him* instead of on men, the development of understanding of what is "of the flesh" and what is "of the Spirit." All these things have taken time and have not come without pain and personal cost.

And it's an *unfinished* process, even after three years.

When these changes led through the roughest of experiences, I sometimes thought of going back to the old way of doing it. I could *never* do it! The life I've found personally – and the life I see in "my people" – is too real, too precious to give up for the security of the old, more acceptable style of church life and pastoral ministry.

I remember that in those early days of change, three years ago, Carl and I would often express how *afraid* we were as we made plans to seek to develop a truly renewed church and to try to build our spiritual babies into mature believers who could find their own ministries. We thought often of the members and attenders of Our Heritage, who would be certain to be "turned off" by the teaching approach and the emphasis on personal discipleship and deep involvement with one another. We visualized a loss of *fifty percent or more* as we de-programmed and started dishing out meat instead of milk on Sunday mornings. And we were scared.

One of us made the statement and the other agreed, "We will lose most of our people and may lose our jobs . . . but then, the way they are and the way we are, *what do we have to lose?*"

V

THOU SHALT NOT "SWEAT" IT

It would have been nice if, during those early days of change, we could have borrowed Cinderella's fairy god-mother to wave her magic wand over our program, priorities and preaching, instantly transforming us all – pastors and people – into renewed Christians living and working together in a sparkling new kind of church fellowship.

But magic wands were as scarce as fairy god-mothers when we began our adventure in renewal.

And in God's real world where institutions are set in their ways, habits are hard to break, men have free will and faith is a *walk*, change requires time. Time for study. Time to re-evaluate everything. Time for the chastening of the Lord. Time for teaching and experimenting. Time for learning new concepts. Time to make the emotional and spiritual adjustments necessary to be able to discard old principles and embrace new ones.

It's not easy to move in a new world where nothing is sacred just because "we've always done it this way." It can make you feel decidedly insecure. It is difficult for a man to admit that many of his highly valued priorities are out of whack. Tough to admit that many of his cherished pastoral goals have been standing in God's way for his whole ministerial life!

It takes time and experience to learn to distinguish the good from the best, the flesh from the Spirit, the wood, hay and stubble from the gold, silver and precious stones. [1]

[1] 1 Corinthians 3:12, 13.

No one can give this kind of training except the Holy Spirit. And the training process is slowed by the fact that I am so accustomed to listening to *men's* opinions, *men's* ideas and *men's* traditions that it is hard to recognize the instructions of the Spirit. Accepting and obeying the Spirit's instructions is harder still. Because, invariably, when the Spirit instructs me, it turns out that I have been doing something *wrong*. And that's hard for my ego to swallow.

The people I live with in the church tend to choke on it, too.

We have all had it drilled into our heads that "the Lord helps them that help themselves" (Hezekiah 8:12).* In addition, we have been programmed by our parents, relatives, schools and social system to succeed. We have been impregnated with the conviction that to "succeed" is to get bigger and bigger and more complicated and to make a bigger splash!

If *we* don't do it, no one will. It's up to us.

Even evangelical churches that preach "grace"[2] give the distinct impression that Christ can save a man's soul and give what help He can, but holy living, witnessing and church building is "up to us."

So, conscientious churches and their pastors, confronted by the Great Commission and feeling guilty from comparing themselves with *The Acts of the Apostles,* spend most of their time trying in vain, by means of sheer human effort, organization and whipping up "enthusiasm," to produce what those *Acts* people had spontaneously in the energy of and under the leadership of the Spirit of God!

It's hard to take any other approach.

Every book for pastors contains more clever ideas for *doing it ourselves*.

Every Christian college and seminary aims at sending out ministers steeped in the glorious institutional idea that through enough hard work, clever manipulation of church members, effective organization and the profuse use of new ideas to "get 'em involved" – "*you too can be a success.*" (Incidentally, God will *help* you.)

Every ministerial convention is more of the same. The pastors

[2]Ephesians 2:8, 9.

*Sorry, no such statement can be found in Scripture. The book of "Hezekiah" doesn't exist!

of the big, successful churches are there to tell you how it's done, how to organize, promote, advertise, preach and handle people so that *"you too can be a success."* At such meetings, the air is literally electrified with great ideas and challenge, challenge, challenge.

A friend of mine came back from a ministerial convention recently with the comment, "I'm so challenged, I'm limp!"

To put into operation the wonderful ideas gleaned from just one ministerial convention would take the next five years! And each idea would probably work. Attendance would increase. Membership would grow. Offerings would swell. Involvement would reach a fever-pitch. Success would be assured.

But the explosive, spontaneous life experienced by the New Testament Church would be no nearer than it was *before* the convention convened!

But *"everybody's* doing it." It's the way to build a big church and to be a "successful minister." The accepted, approved, humanly desirable way. Guaranteed to bring much glory to the pastor, his local church, and the denomination whose "glorious distinctives" he is seeking to spotlight.

Bigness is *the* mark of church success. Big buildings, bulging membership lists and burgeoning budgets are the goals of us all in the modern Madison Avenue approach to building churches. Statistics are almost sacred. Mathematical growth is terribly important to our self-image as pastors.

I've never been asked to fill out a report evaluating the spiritual depth of my people. Or their prayer life. Or the effectiveness of their personal ministries with one another. Or their ability to permeate the community with the influence of Christ. Or the spontaneity of their spiritual life. Or their confidence and poise in the face of difficulty.

Bigness is "where it's at"! And, man, do you have to struggle with your conscience, your feelings of personal worth, your sense of well-being if your church isn't big or getting bigger. It's tough to feel like a failure. To be driven by false guilt. To have to rationalize and make excuses. To hold your head up in confidence in the "awesome presence" of the pastors of the big, successful churches.

It makes you do all manner of compensatory things, like blaming the laymen, the denomination, the devil, or the "fact" that "the world doesn't really want the old fashioned truth anymore."

This whole "numbers game" has gotten out of hand. The New Testament reports numbers, but you have to hunt for them among the pages and pages of *far more important* information, instructions and spiritual goals for church life.

It takes time to adopt a new set of values and to begin striving for new goals that have almost nothing to do with numerology. It's especially difficult when, as you dare to move away from the traditional church "norm," your ministerial colleagues and lay leaders look at you as if you've lost touch with the hard realities of church life.

Even though we were certain to incur the disfavor and the have-you-lost-your-mind looks of some people, we made the decision to try to restructure Our Heritage Church and to change our approach to ministry and church life.

Soon, changes began to take place that practically guaranteed disfavor and statistical losses.

Pet programs began to disappear.

Preaching patterns changed from flashy evangelistic sales pitches to the solid food of Biblical exposition – teaching.

Organizational periphera began to dwindle, leaving less people "involved" in the church machinery.

Believers were told that *they,* not the pastors or the evangelism committee, were chiefly responsible for winning people of the community to Christ.

And each of these changes brought about negative reaction from individuals in the church. Several were convinced that these changes would result in disastrous losses for the church. Some were sure the pastors were leading the church *away* from evangelism and soul-winning toward a program designed solely for people who were already Christians.

One Saturday, thirteen months after our search for God's Living Church began, I had an especially volatile exchange over these things with a strong lay leader who said he spoke for several others in the church. It was an unhappy confrontation. But God, as is His usual habit, used it.

Beside showing me how much I was still walking in the flesh, this confrontation forced me to sit down and think through just what I was trying to do to my church. I pulled together the Biblical principles that had come to guide our new approach to our life together. And as I did, I became more certain than ever that we were on the right track. I became more solidly committed to it.

I laid aside my prepared sermon for the next morning and, instead, presented these principles in what I called *A Defense of My Ministry*. It came at a crucial time and helped both the church and me to get a new grip on our new sense of direction.

I began by asserting my basic position as a minister of the Gospel.

> I am not an *employee* of the church. I was called of God to the ministry and sent by the Holy Spirit to Scottsdale where He has confirmed my ministry with the fruit of men and women turning to Christ. I am bound by unconditional surrender to look to God for guidance in planning the ministry of the church and my preaching. While I am called to serve men, I do not have to please men. But I must please God who sent me.
>
> But those whom I serve certainly have every right to question both what I do and what I preach.
>
> Therefore, so that there will be no lack of clarity, and so that you will know what direction my ministry here must take, I want to pull together the basic philosophy behind the new direction the church and my ministry have been taking lately. I believe this philosophy to be based on the clear scope of New Testament teaching.
>
> This message should hold no surprises since this basic philosophy has been presented in various ways in many sermons over the past thirteen months.

Church life in the New Testament was built around these principles. They did not have to concentrate on them like we do, because they didn't need renewal like we do. They didn't know how to do it any other way. It was the plan the Lord Himself had given them during His years with them in the flesh.

These seven principles of New Testament church life have guided Our Heritage Church as she has sought to rediscover in century twenty the vibrant life of the Christian fellowship of century one:

1. Depend on the Holy Spirit instead of "the flesh."
2. Concentrate on the maturing of Christians.
3. Recognize the priesthood of all believers.
4. Build the church fellowship around *Christ.*
5. Release church life from the confines of the church building.
6. Recognize our place in the total Body of Christ.
7. Build church unity on the basis of love.

Depend on the Holy Spirit instead of "the flesh."

The church in history seems to have thrived under persecution. Perhaps the reason for this is that in extreme persecution many of the earthly, fleshly, human things Christians depend on instead of Christ are taken away so they can no longer be depended on. Since there is nowhere else to turn, the church turns to *God!* In dependence on Him, it rediscovers the life and spiritual power its first century counterpart knew.

What a pity it has to wait until the Lord has allowed all its dear trinkets and crutches to be torn away by force or societal change before it will trust what it should have been trusting all along!

Its living Lord Jesus Christ filling the lives of surrendered people is all the church *really* needs to fulfill its mission in the world. But most of us are quite blind – stubbornly unwilling to see that as the truth.

It just isn't the way things are done.

"The flesh" is represented by all the human, earthly things we expect to produce growth, maturity, spirituality and life in the church – instead of looking to the Holy Spirit for these things.

For instance, in my ministry before our commitment to renewal, I depended on "involvement" in the organization to produce spiritual maturity. The most mature Christian, I was sure, would be the one most "involved" in the committees and activities of the church.

Evangelism depended on my "Sunday sales pitches" and invitations at the end of my sermons. Personal evangelism depended on training, careful organization and consistently applied pastoral pressure.

A great church was dependent on great human leadership, a great program that "involved" everyone in sight, great speaking, great music and a great number of people available to fill all the teaching positions, committees and work assignments that grew out of my great ideas. And surrounding all this and enhancing it must be the finest facilities the congregation can possibly afford (or perhaps even a little finer than that!).

My point is not that any of these things is sinful in itself, or that God cannot use them . . . But I know by what has gone on inside my own head and by what I observe in my ecclesiastical colleagues that these are the things most of us are depending on to build the church, fulfill the Great Commission and mature the saints.

I talked about the Spirit, about trusting God, but proceeded to do everything depending on what *I* could do or devise, and depending heavily upon the people I could get "involved."

. . . Until I found myself trying to talk myself out of the persistent, nagging notion that the whole church and everything in it could be explained easily in terms of human efforts and human ingenuity (mostly mine!). The idea persisted that much about Our Heritage with all its early marks of success was *no miracle at all!* It wasn't *Acts.* It was a monument to the kind of good things men can do . . . *all by themselves.*

If we churchmen are honest, we know in our hearts that most of what we are doing to build our churches is geared to appeal to the carnal mind. [3] We build, plan and preach to the likes and dislikes of the *spiritually immature.* We carefully pamper touchy saints. We feel we can't pay the bills unless we do. *"That's only being realistic."*

[3] 1 Corinthians 3:1-3, Romans 8:5-7.

We depend on buildings. Someone diagnosed our obsession with them as an "edifice complex."

There were no hang-ups in this department in century one. They didn't know the wonderful truth that "it's good for a congregation to be in debt." There simply were no church buildings until after Emperor Constantine ended the persecutions under which the church had thrived for two and one-half centuries and flooded the Christian ranks with baptized pagans in about A.D. 300.

How could those early believers possibly turn the world upside down [4] without church buildings?

In Century One, unschooled fishermen, [5] reformed confidence men, [6] and cooled right-wing revolutionaries [7] who had been with Jesus taught the others. In every Christian group, the Spirit gave gifts and leaders. [8] The church was so completely dependent on the Holy Spirit, it could never have made it without Him.

How did they ever get organized enough to reach whole provinces [9] and entire cities [10] without trained professionals at the helm?

What about the Holy Spirit? Where does He fit into all this?

Usually, in our approach to things, He is sanctimoniously invited to bless what we've already planned, and asked to help in the things we cannot do for ourselves.

But what we are *depending* on is the Sunday school, the sanctuary, the pastor, the Saturday newspaper ad, the sermon, the choir, the board, the ushers, the visitation teams, the greeters, the teachers, the sidewalk sign, the liturgy, the social, the rally, the camping program, the heavy schedule of activities, the "revival" meeting, the clever communications piece, the new idea or program or leader or organ or classroom building or. . . .

[4] Acts 17:6.
[5] Matthew 4:18-22, Acts 4:13.
[6] Luke 5:27-32, Levi is better known as Matthew.
[7] Matthew 10:4, Margin: "Simon, the Zealot." The Zealots were a group of Jewish Nationalists seeking to overthrow Roman rule by force.
[8] 1 Corinthians 12:4-11, 28-30, Ephesians 4:11.
[9] Acts 19:10.
[10] Acts 9:35.

It is tough (!) to let go of all those handfuls of earthly sand we are clawing for and clinging to for dear life and growth and edification, and to begin clinging to the Rock – the *Source* of the things that build the spiritual church.

Caught in the swirling sand of human, fleshly church "necessities," it is difficult to realize that the Spirit is *not* doing it – *we are!*

He will do what He can as an "add-on" to our programs and plans. Romans 8:28 will operate in spite of our willful or stupid or blind occupation of the place that belongs to Him. But only as the Holy Spirit is allowed His place as the actual *Head of the Church, Lord, All in all*, will the Church of the Seventies begin to have any similarity to the Church of *The Acts*. Only as we see Him, and not ourselves, as the church's source of Life, leadership and energy to do its task, will our churches ever rise above the miserable limitations of our own human abilities, talents and intelligence, to become something clearly identifiable as *a work of God*.

Until we come to real dependence on the Spirit of God in us and among us, and to a cessation of our dependence on what the flesh can do, the work of the church will always seem frustrating, weak and riddled with the diseases that plague all human institutions. Until we start to walk and live and operate our churches by faith on Him alone, there will be all too much about our churches that declare them to be little more than the frail efforts of dedicated *men*, trying to do something all by themselves and then, in vain, trying to convince the world and themselves that "*God did it*"!

All that is real, all that is "New Testament," all that is genuinely alive in our local fellowship has come about as we have falteringly, with many lapses in our faith, sought to repudiate our own ability to do anything about it, [11] and have stepped aside to let the Holy Spirit show us what He can do.

It seems strange that Christians have to be told the Holy Spirit can be trusted. Somehow the message hasn't come through from

[11] John 15:5.

the Bible that you don't have to give men and women who are "plugged in" to Him a set of rules and regulations to make them be good.[12] It is clear in the Scriptures that the Spirit will teach,[13] guide into all truth,[14] glorify Christ,[15] convince men,[16] reveal Christ to men,[17] fill men,[18] empower the church,[19] lead its leaders and members,[20] illuminate the Bible to the believing mind,[21] organize the church program,[22] direct church affairs,[23] solve church problems,[24] discipline and chasten,[25] give untrained men the ability to minister,[26] enable men to love each other,[27] unify believers,[28] edify,[29] produce growth,[30] draw people into the Body,[31] meet financial needs,[32] recruit workers,[33] heal minds and bodies,[34] purge and purify,[35] witness,[36] overcome human weakness,[37] increase the effectiveness of prayer,[38] confirm Christ's work in men's hearts. . . .[39] The truth is, the Holy Spirit can

[12] Hebrews 10:16.
[13] John 15:26.
[14] John 16:13.
[15] John 16:14.
[16] John 16:8.
[17] Matthew 16:17.
[18] Acts 2:4, Ephesians 5:18.
[19] Acts 1:8, 4:33.
[20] Acts 16:6-7.
[21] 2 Corinthians 3:14-17, 1 Corinthians 2:14-16.
[22] Acts 13:2.
[23] Acts 15:28.
[24] Philippians 4:19.
[25] Hebrews 12:5-11.
[26] Acts 4:13.
[27] Romans 5:5.
[28] Ephesians 4:3.
[29] 1 Corinthians 12:7.
[30] Ephesians 4:16.
[31] Acts 2:47.
[32] Acts 4:31-35.
[33] Acts 13:2.
[34] Acts 5:16.
[35] Acts 5:1-11, 13.
[36] Acts 1:8 and compare the lives of the disciples in the gospels and after Pentecost (Acts 2).
[37] Romans 8:26.
[38] Romans 8:26.
[39] Romans 8:16.

be trusted to provide the church with *all it needs* to function as the New Testament reveals it should and can.

True, He does these things in and through *men* – but *He* must be the one to do it!

The hardest and most exciting thing we are learning is the near-lost truth that the Holy Spirit can be trusted. He will build the church into a Living Body if we will simply stop trying to do His thing for Him – and *let Him do it!*

Everything the Bible says about Him is true. And when the Spirit does it, it is beautiful.

The pastors of Our Heritage made one rather drastic rule for our ministry as we began to try to get out of the way and let the Spirit do it.

> "Anything in the church program that cannot be maintained without constant pastoral pressure on people to be involved should be allowed to die a sure and natural death."

Three choirs died within two months! Along with mid-week service and several committees. Within eighteen months, the Women's Missionary Society was gone – we were down to one business meeting of any kind each month and another choir was about to bite the dust.

We have approached new ideas and programs with this in mind. Some have succeeded. Many never got past the first meeting. Some were supposedly exploded on the launching pad. We have honestly tried to stick with the commitment that, if God doesn't do it, we are not going to force it to happen over His head.

The people of the church are no longer surprised to hear the pastor announce that some scheme of his has been junked because the Spirit wasn't interested in it and it could only come off if it were pushed through and carried on by large doses of ego-motivated human effort.

I'm concerned about my "face" just like any other man. But painful as it is, it is better for the pastor to "lose face" than to save it at the expense of wasting the whole church's time and effort spent in bringing off something that in the end would be, at best, only wood, hay and stubble.

I'm stubborn, rebellious. I learn slowly.

For example, I am concerned about the Great Commission. So, during the past three years, I have planned evangelism thrust after evangelism thrust. Visitation programs, training sessions, little schemes loaded with law to get reluctant Christians to get out and share their faith in Christ. But reminded by our "let it die" rule, I've filed them all for the better part of three years, waiting for something resembling a green light from the Spirit working in the Body.

My overactive conscience told me I was a shirker. (A few people suggested the idea, too.) But "wait" seemed to be the signal from the Divine Quarterback. "Trust Me," was the message through the Word.

Then, from small groups of Christians throughout the church body came reports of people finding Christ in homes. Reports came of witnessing happening spontaneously across the back fence, at the office and at school.

Then, requests began to come from Christians who had just begun to notice their neighbors and the Lord's Commission, saying, "Pastor, show us how to share Christ with these people."

My green light was shining. At least for evangelism training. And, even without the training, evangelism is taking place. Spontaneously. In the Spirit.

And slowly I'm learning to rest. To trust. To wait. [40]

Our experience in Scottsdale, embryonic as it is, has shown us how the Holy Spirit can handle any situation in the church, if He is trusted with it.

We have seen Him at work, working all things together for good, using problems, pressures and even failures to help make us over into His Son's likeness as a church. [41] We have trusted Him even in situations which we might formerly have viewed as cause for alarm or motivation for a campaign to solve things in the flesh. We've seen Him using such situations for our good.

[40] Psalms 37:7; 62:5; Proverbs 20:22; Hosea 12:6; Isaiah 40:28-31; 49:23; Lamentations 3:25.

[41] Romans 8:28-29.

We have watched, or participated, as the Spirit has dealt with problems between people.

He has beautifully shown Himself to be adequate to solve problems with false teachers who tried to enter our fellowship and disrupt it.

We have sought to depend on the Spirit in matters of outward holiness (smoking, drinking, "worldly" entertainments, attendance at worship, prayer, giving, witnessing, attitudes, prejudices, relationships). The Spirit in the believer and speaking through the Word and the Body is dependable. He doesn't always deal with these matters in the order *we* would choose. Sometimes we wonder if He is dealing with them at all. But the Spirit can be trusted to make whatever changes in Christians He knows are needed, according to His own timetable. And when He does it, it's beautiful. The man is *genuinely changed,* not just conformed to some humanly-devised box we have designed to stuff him into.

We have watched the Holy Spirit silence or remove divisive people and situations that had us worried and fretting. In His way and on His schedule (seldom according to our plans) He has handled, changed, solved or removed the forces of division, seeking to make us "one in the Spirit."

He has stopped us when we were getting ahead of Him and the people. Chastened us when we stubbornly or stupidly went ahead without Him. Pushed when we lagged behind.

He has provided leadership, people, volunteers. Many of the most active and fruitful workers in the church volunteered for their jobs — associate pastor, youth director, junior high director, church secretaries, musicians and several teachers, group leaders etc. They said they felt the Lord leading them to do these things, so they volunteered.

Depending on the Spirit inevitably and invariably involves learning to *wait.* To stop our own activity and wait for His.

When certain areas of traditional church activity "go begging" (choir, clubs, visitation); and certain jobs go undone for weeks (the broken window, the weedy planter, the unpainted door);

and a desirable degree of excellence, finesse and preparedness is lacking in the doing of certain tasks – waiting is difficult.

Frequently, we still find ourselves impatiently trying to do the Lord's work for Him. It is in those times He teaches us some of His most effective lessons in waiting. Like the time Audrey and I planned a "paint party." We just couldn't wait any longer to get the job done. Sixty-seven personal invitations invited more than one hundred-thirty people to the party. We bought gallons of ice cream and makin's for "goo-it-yourself" sundaes . . . *One man showed up to paint!*

In Acts 1:4, Jesus was getting ready to leave. The cloud that was to lift Him into heaven was forming above to envelop Him.

He had trained and shared with these men for three years. He had just told them that they were commissioned to make disciples of people everywhere. After seeing Him alive from the dead, they were convinced that He was the Messiah, Savior and Son of God. They had a fantastic story to tell.

Here was impetuous, impatient Peter. Hot-blooded Simon the Zealot was there. And those ambitious sons of thunder, James and John. Levi, the tax collector, a shortcut expert if there ever was one.

Waiting was simply not their bag. They were men of action. Men with drive. Men with ideas and solutions. They all had active adrenalin glands.

But Jesus' instructions read: "Wait!" [42]

Wait for God's promise. Wait for the Spirit. Don't try anything – not one testimony or sermon or evangelistic crusade or missionary journey. Don't plan anything – not one scheme designed to carry out the Lord's command.

Wait! Until you are filled with the Spirit.

Wait! Until God takes control of you.

Wait! Until He begins to do the work through you.

Waiting isn't easy. If we are going to trust Him to do it for us and in us and through us, we can't do it with an alternate plan in mind in case the Spirit's program doesn't come off on our preannounced time schedule.

[42] Acts 1:4.

Audrey paraphrases Proverbs 3:5, 6 to fit the way most of us operate:

> "Trust in the Lord with all thine heart . . . and keep a plan in the back of your mind in case that doesn't work!"

The personal result of a church trying to depend on the Holy Spirit in all the situations of its life is that its people and its leaders discover what it is to *rest*.

Jesus' words have new meaning: "Come unto me all ye that labor . . . and I will give you *rest*."[43]

No more struggling and worrying. Except when you forget or willfully grab the ball again and start running with it, independently. When that happens, if you've once tasted rest, you cannot live long without it. You've got to "let go and let God" again. So you can be at rest.

From this new point of view, the message of the New Testament, with its Spirit-filling,[44] its faith-walking,[45] and its "Christ-in-you" hope,[46] is like adding an eleventh commandment to the Mosaic Decalog, which, in the words of an Our Heritage cliché would read:

"Thou Shalt Not 'Sweat' It!"

There is wonderful release from pressure and tension when, as a pastor, or layman, you discover that the Holy Spirit is in His Church and that He can be trusted to provide for all it needs to really be a *living* church. That He can be trusted to carry out *through* it all its Living Head commissions it to do.

My experience with seeking to build a church through dependence on the Spirit instead of "*the flesh*" is limited and brief. But already I have seen enough to be convinced that the church will be strongest when it is willing purposely to put itself into the position, organizationally and otherwise, where it will collapse if the Spirit doesn't move in and keep it alive.

[43] Matthew 11:28.
[44] Ephesians 5:18.
[45] 2 Corinthians 5:7.
[46] Colossians 1:27.

VI

THE PRINCIPLE OF THE THING

When you start trying to reinstate Christ as Head of the Church, in a practical sense, you sometimes get the feeling that you're suddenly in a sort of ecclesiastical "no-man's land." All the traditional sources of authority and direction and ideas for running the church begin gathering dust on your library shelves.

I can't even remember the titles of many books I once reached for every week for "answers" to this or that problem.

When you start to move away from trying to build an institution around the best ideas the human mind can create, to start looking for a church life which leans on the Holy Spirit for wisdom, direction, and continuity, your personal ministry may literally be turned upside down.

You discover yourself out on a limb with nothing to hang on to but the Word of God and leadership of His Spirit.

As I began to creep hesitantly out on that limb, leaving behind the "safety" of what had become accepted and usual and "normal" in the church, the Word and the Spirit began to make radical changes in my concept of how a church operates. Along with different goals, I discovered that there would need to be a revolution in our approach to reaching the new goals.

Structures, forms, purposes, preaching, organization and areas of concentration all seemed, in one degree or another, to be missing the mark the Word sets forth.

Most difficult to face was the fact that a different kind of pastoral ministry than my church presently had was demanded of me.

The flesh rebelled against these things. Surely, "10,000 Bible-believing clergymen can't be wrong!" My mind, steeped in the traditions of the evangelical status quo, argued that the New Testament's approach could never work today.

"That was A.D. 33 — this is the space age. Space-age evangelism and ministry in the seventies calls for more sophistication. Surely, we've learned *something* of value in 2000 years. Our Madison Avenue methods are *right for us*. They are what *God is blessing* today.

"If we tried to do it the way they did," I reasoned, "evangelism would suffer, the professional ministry would suffer, my denomination would suffer, much that we count as progress would suffer, finances would suffer, and there would be too much freedom from needed pastoral control. Things would get out of hand!"

Those were my *first* thoughts. My *second* thought was, "Wow! I'd love to see *that — the church getting out of hand!*"

All the sophistication and so-called "up-to-date" approaches to church life have not given us that glorious a church! We have been given some *big* churches. Some *growing* churches. Some beautiful church buildings. Some gigantic, efficient and influential organizations. But we look in vain for any but fleeting glimpses of the spontaneous life and spiritual power of those unsophisticated believers of Century One.

"Lord, lead me to that. If it doesn't work, at least we will have given it a chance and can warn the world to stay in its rut!"

So . . . the Lord began to lead us to it. He gave us seven principles of New Testament Church life as stars by which to set our course.

In the previous chapter, I spelled out the first and most important of the seven:

Depend on the Holy Spirit instead of the flesh.

If the church is to experience and share spontaneous, overflowing life in the Spirit, it can never come to such life by the manipulations and struggles of the flesh. "That which is born of the flesh is flesh (it can't be anything else); and that which is born of the Spirit is spirit" — Jesus.[1]

Then. . .

Concentrate on the maturing of Christians.

One of the more ingenious tricks the devil has played on us "conservative, evangelical, fundamentalist, Bible-believing Christians" has been to get us to confuse what we should be doing when we come together with what we should be doing when we go out into the world.

We have been bedeviled into believing we should be "evangelizing" when we are together (when not more than five percent of those present are non-Christians). And, while "out there in the world," we are taught to be a "separated people," lest we become tainted by the influence of the ungodly should we associate with them too closely.

Consequently, nearly every time he goes to church, the average evangelical Christian hears a simple evangelistic sermon designed to "convert the sinner" (who isn't there). While, "out in the world," he doesn't have three friends who are not Christians.

No question about it. The Great Commission says, "Go ye into all the world and *bring them into the church building,* so the *pastor* can preach the Gospel to every creature."

Pastoral egos are like this. We like to be depended on. It's great to be indispensable to the salvation of the lost, to be the only "professional soul-winner" in the church. So, as long as we see a few people "coming forward," we do not get too concerned by the reproductive sterility of our members. And, we can tell ourselves that a continuous diet of "evangelistic" (elementary-level) preaching is what the church needs. If we are blessed enough to see people "coming forward" several Sundays in a row, we are "having revival," and can *know for sure* we are doing the right thing.

In some weary hour, when we stop to face for an honest, fleeting moment the utter impossibility of thinking that the world could possibly be reached *inside* the church, we may even admit

[1] John 3:6.

that if our members were winning people to Christ, as they ought to be, we might be able to minister differently. But they aren't and won't and can't – so we must go on as we are.

We cannot figure out *why* they don't move past the baby stage into reproduction. The fact that they never get anything but milk from the pulpit and the church program somehow doesn't seem to our ecclesiastical mentality to be relevant to the problem.

Is the purpose of the church, as it comes together, to win the lost? Or do we have our church fellowship confused with our mission in the world?

In the First Century Church, unbelievers became believers at gatherings of the believers, but that does not seem to be the purpose that brought them together. In Acts 2:42-47, the Lord added new converts to the church daily, but the reason for gathering together was so that those who were already believers could be taught by the apostles, enjoy spiritual fellowship with one another, remember the Lord's death and its benefits by sharing communion, and pray together.

As they did this, they began to love each other and to care for each other. They became personal enough with each other to notice their brothers and sisters in need. So they started – spontaneously – sharing everything they had together.

And when the doors opened, and they poured into the streets and market places and neighborhoods, the believers were so excited about the way they were loved, the Life they had to share with the world, and about what God was doing for them, in them, among them and through them, that the people they talked to *spontaneously*, wanted to get in on the happening.

While the unconverted may often have been present at the early Christian meetings of Acts 2, a short time later it became a totally different story. After the sudden deaths of Ananias and Sapphira at a Christian meeting in Acts 5, unbelievers suddenly began staying away in droves! (Acts 5:13). And, amazing as it may seem to us moderns, verse 14 says that in spite of the fact that the unconverted were no longer attending church, *more than ever* were being added to the Lord, "multitudes of both men and women."

Early church gatherings were for Christians to grow – *not* for evangelism. Even though the modern evangelical mind cannot understand, their evangelism was as explosive as it was, in part, because their gatherings were what they were. Their meetings had everything to do with their day-after-day, everybody-doing-it kind of evangelism.

Jesus Himself set the strategy. He preached to large crowds, touched and healed and converted and exorcised hundreds. He preached His Good News of the Kingdom everywhere. And He invited more than did it to follow Him.

But . . .

Most of His time and energy and attention was concentrated on the spiritual development of a small group of men who followed when He called.

They went with Him everywhere. They heard all His sermons – all His teaching. They observed Him under pressure, in need, tired, rejected, accepted, sought for, alone, in temptation, in worship, preaching, praying, loving, healing, casting out demons, answering His enemies, setting His steps toward the cross. Following each public teaching session or confrontation, these few believers were with Him for a deeper explanation of parables, doctrines and divine purposes. When they were alone, He talked about things the world outside would never have understood.

He did not commit Himself to everyone. Most could not receive deeply of Him because of the surface nature of their belief.[2] But He poured Himself deeply into the twelve. They saw Him intimately. They shared His private moments. They knew Him and His message and His mission better than anyone else.

Because that was His plan . . .

To leave behind a small group of people, having complete knowledge of His Person. Who, once filled with His Spirit, could turn the world upside down.[3]

Jesus was an evangelist, but in today's terms, He wasn't a very successful one. After three years, the biggest crowd He

[2] John 2:23-25.
[3] Acts 17:6.

could muster to see Him alive from the dead was 500.[4] And only 120 waited in the upstairs room for the Holy Spirit.[5] But, trying to give a good statistical report wasn't the purpose of His ministry. He aimed to redeem the *whole world* and then to get the word out about it to *every future generation.* So that this might be accomplished, He concentrated on that little knot of believers. He spent most of His time building them, teaching them, maturing them and preparing them for their ministry.

Believers.

The main thrust of His ministry was to *believers.*

The church He founded at Pentecost followed His strategy.

Which of the New Testament Epistles was written to unbelievers?

Not one.

Parts in each are useful in leading pagans to the Savior, but *all* of the New Testament letters have a common basic purpose: *to bring believers to maturity.*

And when the church gathered, its purpose was the same. This is the way Paul described the ministry of the early church:

> His "gifts unto men" were varied. Some He made His messengers, some prophets, some preachers of the gospel; to some He gave the power to guide and teach His people. His gifts were made that Christians might be properly equipped for their service; that the whole body might be built up until the time comes when, in the unity of common faith and common knowledge of the Son of God, we arrive at real maturity—that measure of development which is meant by "the fulness of Christ."
>
> We are not meant to remain as children at the mercy of chance wind of teaching and the jockeying of men who are expert in the crafty presentation of lies. But, we are meant to hold firmly to the truth in love and to grow up in every way into Christ, the head. For it is from the head that the whole body, as a harmonious structure knit together by the joints with which it is provided, grows by the proper functioning of individual parts to its full maturity in love.[6]

[4] 1 Corinthians 15:6.

[5] Acts 1:15.

[6] Ephesians 4:11-16, *The New Testament in Modern English,* by J. B. Phillips, The Macmillan Co. (1965).

When the church comes together it is not to concentrate on converting the five percent who may have dropped in for the services, but it is to concentrate on the maturing, stabilizing, edifying, grounding, deepening, developing, effective living and ministering of its "in-group" believers.

Its ministry is not to be aimed at building the biggest crowd possible, but at building believers (whatever their number) into a vital person-to-person fellowship of love – fellowship that really comes to "know" the Son of God.

The reason more unbelievers could become believers in Acts 5:14, in spite of the fact that unbelievers stopped going to church, is that mature believers, no longer "at the mercy of every chance wind of teaching," who love each other and get to know the Son of God, *witness*. *Spontaneously*. Even without training.

If that is true, then it is no abdication of evangelistic responsibility to stop trying to evangelize when the Body gathers, in order to *concentrate on the maturing of Christians*.

Today I see my ministry chiefly as a ministry to Christians. As an individual believer, I am as responsible to witness and win pagans as any other believer. But, as a pastor, my *first* responsibility is to teach and to structure the church so as to encourage the spiritual growth and maturity of believers until they become able to carry out their own evangelistic responsibilities.

When the church gathers, I see it gathering to be taught the Word, Bible doctrine and the practical application of these things in their lives.

I did not see myself as a teacher until three years ago. In fact, I stayed away from teaching situations as much as possible. They frightened me. And the process of changing from "official church soul-winner" and "P. R. man" to pastor-teacher has been a very painful process for me. It has also been agonizing for the church which has patiently, lovingly endured some of the sad sermonic efforts that have marred the path toward that goal. And the process, the learning how, is not over yet. I still have a lot of learning to do. Like the church, I'm not fully "renewed."

Maturity also comes through experience in ministry. And there it must be "first-things first." Instead of trying to coerce people through condemning their inactivity (hoping the guilt generated will move them to act), laying down the "law" (their "Christian duty"), and creating certain other pressures to force Christians to witness, pray and do the other "Christian things," we have encouraged them to get together in small groups in their homes, where they can study the Bible, exercise spiritual gifts, share their burdens and have opportunities to minister to each other.

There, through sharing the happenings of their lives together, they are discovering the personal, powerful reality of the Living Jesus, and the value to everyday life of personal dependence on the Spirit who lives in them. And maturity is beginning to happen. Believers are beginning to "grow up into Christ, the head" – beginning to take Him into the nitty-gritty of everyday life.

I sit back and watch, in thankful excitement, as hesitatingly, at first in bud form, and then gradually coming to full bloom, witnessing, praying, loving and believing God, begin to happen. *Spontaneously.*

Recognize the priesthood of all believers.

We made a definite decision to go in the direction we have gone seeking renewal. Shortly after making that decision, I began to say publicly:

> "I believe the Lord wants to lead our congregation to the point of spiritual maturity where it can, if need be, function *without a professional pastor.*
>
> "I am no longer going to be this church's 'resident evangelist.' My role has to change to pastor-teacher. If people are to be brought to Christ, from now on *you* will have to do it. It is no longer my 'job.'
>
> "And, not only that, we must come to realize that this church has more than one minister. You have depended too long on the ministry of one man. I've helped to teach you to do that. But now I see that God has given *every* believer in Christ a ministry to the other members of the Body. Until each of us begins to find his ministry, the church will never really be healthy. As long as the congregation looks only

> to its pastor for life and ministry, we will never experience the kind of fellowship the New Testament Church experienced, and our life together will never be full and abundant as God intended it to be."

Individual Christians are supposed to be evangelists and ministers in the church. These tasks were never intended to be the work of a handful of professionals.

In Christ's plan for His church, every person whom He receives receives Him. At the moment Christ is received, the Holy Spirit moves in to live in the person's life.[7] And, when the Spirit comes in, the believer is placed into the Body of Christ,[8] and is given certain spiritual gifts[9] according to the will of the Spirit[10] – gifts to be used in each Christian's personal ministry to other members of the Body and to the Body as a whole.[11]

In the Spirit's design for the church, every believer is ordained a priest.[12] St. Jerome called baptism "the ordination of the laity."

Every Christian, having the Life of Christ in him, is equipped for a personal ministry to his fellow believers[13] and to unbelievers.[14]

All evangelicals agree with the *theory*. Every college course on church history credits Martin Luther with having revived "the priesthood of believers." We all recognize the existence of this priesthood – except that we make no provision for it in the structure of our churches.

Where is there a place for this priesthood ministry to operate in most churches? In the Wednesday night testimony meeting, where we are bored to numbness hearing the same dry testimonies every week? In the Sunday school class, where only one person (the teacher) is allowed to exercise his gift? The only one who

[7] Romans 8:9, 1 Corinthians 12:3.
[8] 1 Corinthians 12:13.
[9] 1 Corinthians 12:7-10, 28-31, Ephesians 4:11, Romans 12:6-8.
[10] 1 Corinthians 12:11.
[11] 1 Corinthians 12:7.
[12] 1 Peter 2:5, 9; Revelation 1:6.
[13] Ephesians 4:16.
[14] Acts 1:8.

functions as priest and minister in the worship services is the pastor. (Though I suppose, in the technical sense, we can claim priestly ministry for the organist, singers and ushers.) But, as one pastor said when asked by one of his members what he could do to serve the Lord, "I really don't know! We already have twenty ushers!"

Luther's emphasis, and Peter's in First Peter 2 and Paul's in Ephesians 4, is on "the priesthood of all believers."

All.

The glimpse into an early church meeting in Corinthians indicates that all were free, under the Spirit's leadership and the laws of orderliness, to minister with the gifts the Spirit had given.

> What then, brethren, is the right course? When you meet together, each one has a hymn, a teaching, a disclosure of special knowledge or information, an utterance in a strange tongue or an interpretation of it. But, let everything be constructive and edifying and for the good of all.[15]

The "all-believers" priesthood of the church in century one is also glimpsed in Hebrews 10:24 and 25. This "assembling" isn't a "one-man show." It is a "one another" ministry.

> And, let us consider and give attentive, continuous care to watching over one another, studying how we may stir up (stimulate and incite) to love and helpful deeds and noble activities; not forsaking or neglecting to assemble together as believers, as is the habit of some people, but admonishing — warning, urging and encouraging — one another, and all the more faithfully as you see the day approaching.[16]

I looked around at my church and could not find a single part of the program that would allow for that kind of mutual ministry. We believed in "the priesthood of all believers" as a fine theory. But we did not practice it.

No wonder there were so few of us who could stand on our own two feet spiritually. We were trapped in a one-man, one-gift ministry that never gave opportunity for anyone but the pastor to exercise spiritual muscles. We were as weak and sickly

[15] 1 Corinthians 14:26, *Amplified New Testament.*
[16] Hebrews 10:24-25, *Amplified New Testament.*

as a vitamin and mineral deficient child. There were ministries vital to our health and life that we simply never received because our church structures and forms did not allow for them.

Gifts of the Spirit lay dormant and unused because we gave the Spirit *no opportunity* for their use.

There is much more for us to learn about mutual ministry and the "all-believers priesthood," but it cannot now be said that there is no opportunity for even the weakest believer among us to minister life to the church if he will: the free-wheeling sharing in small groups (which we call "The Little Churches"); the "friendship time" in the Sunday morning meeting (several minutes of informal conversation between people about what's happening in their lives); the completely unstructured Sunday evening meeting; the frequent use of laymen as preachers and teachers in all levels of church life.

Such things can seem foolish and even dangerous, unless one recognizes that the Holy Spirit lives in even the weakest believer. And the Holy Spirit can be trusted to do good things in a spiritual fellowship which *recognizes the priesthood of all believers.*

Build the church fellowship around Christ.

Because we are not really convinced that Christ and His Gospel are enough reason to exist as churches, we develop and fight tenaciously for our "glorious distinctives" and other secondary issues to which we can rally people.

Paul sharply reprimanded the Corinthian Christians for their separating into little denomination-like groupings and then advertizing:

"We are of Paul."

"We are of Apollos."

"We are of Peter."

or . . . "We are of Christ."[17]

Paul diagnosed their problem and declared, "You are of none of these. You are really *of the flesh!*"[18]

[17] 1 Corinthians 1:12.
[18] 1 Corinthians 3:1-4.

It is *Christ* who saves. It is *Christ* who died for our sins. It is *Christ* who gives us eternal life. It is *Christ* who places us into His Body and sets us apart from the world. It is *Christ* who distinguishes us from all other people. *Christ is our glorious distinctive.*

He is enough on which to build a vital church fellowship. No human additives are needed. But still, like the carnal Corinthians, we insist on trying to find some rallying point that appeals to the flesh and its pride.

"We are pre-millennial."

"We have no prophecy hang-up."

"We are 'pre-trib' " . . . " 'mid-trib' " . . . " 'post-trib.' "

"We are historic."

"We are independent."

"We are charismatic."

"We are holiness."

"We are the friendliest church in . . ."

The church Christ came to build is to be built as a fellowship of people around *Him*. A fellowship that rallies around the only, real, living Person of Jesus Christ.

If it has distinctives, it is to be because it is a fellowship of people experiencing His distinctive life, indwelt by His distinctive Spirit and seeking to live distinctively in Him – a fellowship earnestly trying to get to know Him as He really is, to be conformed to His image, and to be obedient to His will.

All the activities, services and gatherings of such a fellowship will have one aim; to enhance relationship to, dependence on, service to and life in the *Personal Jesus*. It will depend on Him for its life. It will not depend on pastor, buildings, program or "distinctives" which appeal only to human pride. And, it will teach its people not to depend on these things, but to depend on Christ for everything. Christ will be the focal point and purpose of all that takes place.

"Truly, our fellowship is with the Father and with his Son Jesus Christ"(1 John 1:3).

If I were able to be totally honest, sometimes I think I would stand up before my congregation and say, "I would *like* to say we have come together to worship and fellowship with Jesus Christ, but the *truth* is that I know we have come to hear the music, be stimulated by the cleverness and emotional impact of a man's rhetoric, enjoy the dim quietness of the sanctuary and to meet our friends.

"We chose *this* church because of the combined appeal of its architecture, its smallness or bigness, its activity schedule, its similarity to 'the church I knew when I was a kid,' its friendliness, and because of the persistent and effective manner of advertising by which it kept its name before me and built its image in my mind as the kind of organization in which I would like to be involved."

If we were honest, we would admit that we really don't think Christ "sells" too well without our added human trappings. He hasn't enough appeal in Himself to do the job. You can't build a church with Christ alone as the focal point of its fellowship. You have to appeal to the flesh, at least to a degree. Especially in America where the competition for church members is so stiff.

A church overly dependent on its buildings would fall apart if it had to suddenly move to rented facilities, into homes, or into hiding for its meetings.

A church overly dependent on its pastor always suffers statistical losses when the pastor moves to another church, or even when he merely goes on vacation.

A church where Christ is the heart-beat of the fellowship – a church in which the all-believer priesthood operates – can be strong and effective with or without a building, a professional pastor and many of the other things in which the flesh finds security and enjoyment and which sometimes become substitutes for simply sharing the Life of Christ together.

In a church built as a fellowship around Jesus Christ, the Spirit Himself will choose and gift leaders, teachers and spiritual counselors from among the priesthood of believers. The rallying point and base of operations will not be the physical facilities, but the fellowship. The catalyst and strong leader will not be a man or a machine but the Living Head of the Church Himself.

It could not happen as long as I kept impressing the church

with my indispensability to it, as the *only* one who knew how to do a myriad of things, the *only* one who ever preached, the *all-knowing* authority on every matter, the *only* "trained professional" counselor, the chairman of everything, the teacher of everything, the one responsible for everything, the one without whose blessing and prompting nobody acts or innovates or leads or does anything! Me: the "great white father," the "all-spiritual high priest," the one-man "whirling dervish" and spiritual tornado, the "little tin god."

It could not happen as long as our "edifice complex" kept us all properly entombed within the concrete confinement of our chapel walls. Which leads us to the fifth principle . . .

Release church life from the confines of the church building.

The early church did not have to be reminded that its ministry was in the world. There was simply nowhere else for it to minister. It knew nothing of architectural wonders of marble, timber and stained glass in which to gather the faithful.

When you said "church" on Monday morning in those days, no one thought you were talking about an empty building. They didn't know any better than to envision *people*. Because that was the only concept they had of "church."

There were no whole congregations concentrating all their energies, time, tithes and pastoral attention on raising thousands for bricks and planks and, later, for mortgages and interest. (All so easily justified, because "it's part of our 'outreach' into the community.")

We pastors and people find it impossible to think "church" without these things. "It can't be done without them," we insist, without even a second thought that there might be another way.

We are steeped in it. It's traditional and has been for a millennium and a half. It's what our communities and our people and our denominational leaders and the whole Christian world expect. You might meet in a home or a school or other borrowed facilities for a while, but that can only be temporary until we get a few people together, buy some land and start a capital funds drive.

In Century One, they did it without all this – and amazingly well, too. But this is a different age, we protest. We've come a long way in 2,000 years!

The truth is, we are trapped inside the "peaked box" we call "a church." It is where people must come to be saved. It's the rallying point that keeps the congregation "together." Our "image in the community" depends on it. It's the center of social life. To enter its warm interior is to "come into the presence of God." He lives there – at the church.

Until three years ago, I had the conviction that one of the keys to a successful church was that the lights be burning at the church every night!

But three years ago, I began to wake up. We began *moving out* of the buildings I had thought were so absolutely important to all of church life.

First, the lights went out on Wednesday night. Midweek service became two small home-based Bible study units ("growth cells," we called them then). One met on Tuesday, the other on Wednesday.

Then, the lights went out on Tuesday. The work of several boards and committees became part of the responsibilities of the Church Board. We were deliberately cutting down the number of nights that were occupied with church busywork.

Then, the lights went out on Monday night. The Women's Missionary Society collasped with a heart-warming crunch, and the women began to gather in daytime home groups to study the Bible, pray and share deeply in life together.

Then, the lights went out on other nights, so that youth activities could move into the homes and three choirs could die from neglect.

Etcetera.

We began gradually, little by little (looking back, it seems to have happened rather fast), to physically decentralize the ministry of the church. To release it from its unhealthy confinement in and dependence on its "plant," its pastors, its "leaders," and its institution.

As we began to scatter the church's ministry throughout the

neighborhood, we released it from the schedule of meetings which had kept its members tied to "Mama-Church's" apron strings. We began to send it out into the real world, to get involved there and to confront and change it.

Recognize our place in the total Body of Christ.

The True Body of Christ, the Spiritual Church, is in no way divided, because:

> "There is *one* body, and *one* Spirit, even as ye are called in *one* hope of your calling; *one* Lord, *one* faith, *one* (spiritual) baptism, *one* God and Father of all . . ." [19]
>
> "For by *one* Spirit are we all baptized into *one* body, whether we be Jews or Gentiles, whether we be bond or free; and have been all made to drink into *one* Spirit." [20]

The Spiritual Church cannot be divided.

But, the organic expression of it on earth is tragically splintered and divided.

I do not believe, however, that the greatest sin is our organizational division. The greatest sin against the Body of Christ is our *attitude* of division.

Certain groups of believers and their leaders think they are Scripturally correct because they have renounced denominationalism as the sin it is and have organized "independent local" churches. They do not realize that "independence" is also intolerable in the Body of Christ. Independence, then, becomes merely a single-church approach to divisiveness. [21]

Many "independent local" churches are nothing more than "one-church denominations." They have not solved the problem of the splintered Body at all. In fact, they have added to the spirit of division.

While I, personally, have come to deplore the effects of denominationalism on the Body and on its presentation of itself to the world (which can't help but be confused and wonder about the quality of our love for one another), I have chosen to remain

[19] Ephesians 4:4-6, KJV (italics mine)
[20] 1 Corinthians 12:13, KJV (italics mine)
[21] 1 Corinthians 1:11-13, 3:3-4.

a member of the denomination which brought me to Christ and has supported Our Heritage Church from the beginning. My conscience will not allow me to splinter the Body further by separating myself or encouraging my church to separate itself from our brothers and sisters in Christ who make up the denomination.

What would we possibly gain?

Independence. But I fail to see that independence has brought independent churches any more of a consciousness of the spiritual world-wide Body of Christ. Everything the Word teaches about the Body indicates that God has put us together into Christ in a relationship that is characterized by dependence on one another, oneness in spirit and need of each other's ministries.

A few organizational mergers are taking place among evangelical denominations, but they are only tokens of the unity we need to recognize. They will never happen fast enough to convince this generation that we are really one. And with each merger comes a certain amount of splintering of dissident churches into independence or tiny new denominations. Thus, the division proliferates.

I favor evangelical denominational merger. I am personally ready to merge all evangelicals, including the independents, into one Bible-believing church.

It's a pipe dream.

It will never happen by organizational processes. The flesh with its pride pretty well assures that. Besides, the monumental organizational structure that would be developed, combining with the human lust for power and recognition would create other problems that would continue to divert attention and energy from the spiritual tasks the church is supposed to be doing.

We know that more – much more – is needed to solve the problem of the divided visible church, but we have begun, at least, to try to view our work as *building the Kingdom of Christ, whether the local church, the denomination or the statistical report increase in number or not.*

It's easier to *say* we will do it than it is to *do* it. But we are attempting to learn how to do our work with the whole Body in view.

We are seeking to win people to the Lord Jesus, to build them up in the faith and be thankful for the privilege – *even* if not one nickel of their tithe ever touches our offering plates. Even if in doing so we build up the Sunday morning congregation of the church they already belonged to B.C., or the evangelical church in their neighborhood that they choose to attend instead of ours.

Our small groups (Little Churches) contain people from other churches, who have come alive in Christ through the ministry of the group, but who still belong to and are more active than ever in a church which failed to bring them to a vital relationship with Christ. And, we rejoice that now that church has a *witness inside.*

We are beginning to learn to rejoice in the fact that *the Kingdom is being built.*

How can we be a "*New Testament* Church" and add to or be a part of the spirit of division among true Christians?

I pray for the day when all who follow Jesus Christ and live by His Gospel can forget their man-made divisions (with all their "hallowed tradition") and can let the political, organizational walls of distrust, disputation and self-righteousness crumble from purposeful neglect. And over the rubble of those broken-down old walls, we'll see each other as interdependent parts of the "*one Body in Christ.*"

Build church unity on the basis of love.

I cannot imagine the members of the early church going dutifully to their religious meetings as little individual islands surrounded by the cold waters of an impersonal image, sitting shoulder to shoulder to hear what was going on at the front, never seeing or being seen by, and never caring for or being cared for by the people with whom they meet.

This *is* the picture of what happens in many Christian congregations today.

In the church of Century One, the one thing that characterized their meetings was soul-fellowship.[22] An intensely personal soul-fellowship that had as its heartbeat a Spirit-ignited, fervent, personal *love*.

It was a *personal* church.

There was too much harsh reality facing believers in the world around them for them to spend time when they came together exchanging pasted-on smiles and soggy handshakes. They had deep, rock-real needs that such *games* could never meet. There were no padded pews, majestic organ strains or expensive altar appointments to help lift their thoughts to that lofty realm of unreality where fuzzy thoughts of God make one feel good, and for a few moments, forget life as it is. In such a setting one can hide from himself and his brothers and still feel that he has done his "religious thing."

Christianity was not "a religion" in the book of Acts. It was *life*. Real. Personal. It dealt with the facts as they are and with life as it is.

It met its constituents at a need level. At the level of *real* needs.

It was a personal church. You knew your brother. You knew his hurts and his needs. And he knew yours. You ministered to him spiritually and physically. And he ministered to you.

You didn't hide in your favorite pew and slip out unnoticed. You were confronted eyeball to eyeball. You were noticed. Reached out to. *Loved*. Not as one of a "congregation," but as *one person*.

It was a *personal* church.

Ours wasn't. And, the coffee we drank together and the "fellowship suppers" and the "involvement" with one another in church business and church programming wasn't making it happen.

I knew we were impersonal (but no more than any other evangelical church). "Most people like it that way," I told myself. "If we started getting too personal we'd scare a lot of people off!"

But love wasn't happening.

The opposites of it showed up from time to time. But, the New

[22] Koinonia, Acts 2:42.

Testament soul-fellowship could not happen – no matter how hard I preached it and no matter how many "fellowship suppers" I planned. I did not even realize that our approach to worship and to church life provided no point at which people were given a setting in which to break out of the impersonal shells which encased them or to get inside the shell of another where soul-fellowship can happen. A few people found it in spite of this lack. But it was the exception.

Now . . . we are getting *personal.*

Today, if you come to our meetings (even the Sunday morning "worship service") you can't hide. You will talk to someone. You will look into someone's face. You will give someone your name. You will become initially acquainted with someone, and they with you, because you have engaged in conversation. It's called "Friendship," and it is included in the "order of service" (we haven't gotten away from that yet).

Meeting each other is not love, but it has led to friendships and to fellowship. It's a start. It's *personal.* A few people have felt threatened by it. Most have expressed great pleasure in it.

Soul-fellowship also blossoms when the people get to know each other in the personal informality of small groups. They begin to watch out for each other, visit each other when sickness or problems come, laugh or weep with one another, step in to solve material needs when they occur, pray for each other and bear one another's burdens, hang-ups and sins.

In *love.*

In genuine *caring* fellowship.

These seven basic New Testament principles of church life have been the foundation for the mini-revolution we are experiencing, a revolution we expect to continue experiencing.

Constantly confronting us are some additional areas of church life to which we have not yet applied these principles. The "how to" usually comes after an extended period of prayer and heart-searching in the light of the Word of God.

The Lord is gradually changing us. We have been given a few glimpses of the church He wants to build. Until – now – we *want* to be changed.

No one realizes any better than I do that these principles, gleaned from study of church life in the New Testament, cut squarely across many of the "tried and true" tenets of the modern-day philosophy of church development. I have probably overlooked some other important principles. Human reasoning naturally argues that many things that are absolutely essential to church success have been left out (i.e., finances, advertising and promotion, organizational structure, etc.). Even the New Testament deals with some of these things.

But . . .

I am firmly convinced that these are, to some extent, incidental to church life, and that, in the average church, these incidentals have been blown 'way out of proportion – to the detriment and deterioration of the vital church Jesus came to build.

I don't believe God left anything solely "up to us," in the planning of the church. His Word contains principles that apply to every need the church has or will ever have.

The important thing is to face the fact that the flesh has made nearly disastrous inroads into church life and has, sometimes through *centuries* of church history, become firmly entrenched there. I am praying for the kind of heavenly dynamite that will be needed to blast your church and mine free from the debilitating clutches of the flesh and set the church moving along a high way of spiritual advance where it looks to the Holy Spirit *alone* for all it needs to begin to become, once again . . .

God's Church!

VII

GOALS FOR AN IDEAL CHURCH

SEVEN MONTHS of learning and spiritual conflict followed the presentation of the "Seven Principles of New Testament Church Life" to the congregation.

Opposition to this "new approach" grew. To some of our leaders, de-programming was displeasing. Some parents complained about the loss of the children's choirs (which died simply from lack of interest, not by pastoral design. Though pastoral design did decide not to fight to maintain anything that could not survive without pastoral pressure). A few charter members reminded me of "the days when" . . . this program, or that rally, or this social event, or that contest was so successful and enjoyable. Sunday school constituents who had come for "the loaves and the fishes" of some man-made promotional scheme began to absent themselves when the frolic of clever promotion began to fade out. And some worship attenders who had previously enjoyed hearing flashy sermons on elementary truth, began to go church-shopping again when the sermons started to require some chewing for proper digestion. (Though, I suppose, they can't be entirely blamed for giving up. For, as I mentioned earlier, some of those sermons preached during my period of transition from evangelistic preaching to pastoral teaching were pretty depressing – even to me!)

Then, a few lay leaders, already somewhat disenchanted with the turn of affairs the church was taking, began to notice that so-and-so wasn't around anymore. "What have you done to try to keep him?" they asked.

Statistical reports struggled to keep pace with "last year," and then began to slip behind. I'm sure my appeal that we are trying to accomplish *more important things* than just to set new records must have had the hollow sound of an empty excuse. (I will have to admit that I, myself, had to struggle psychologically with the statistical losses.)

Irritations and disputes characterized several of our business meetings during that seven months. I did not always have a ready Biblical answer for every objection or for the suggestion that the direction the church was now headed might be a colossal mistake. I was finding my way in this new territory, too.

The new emphasis on walking in dependence on the Spirit instead of the pressure of "laying down the law" was blamed for every lack in offerings, every Sunday school teaching vacancy, and every decrease in attendance.

The opposition was limited to a minority, albeit a very strong and vocal minority. Most of the "involved" church members were in sympathy with the direction we were going. Some were even excited about it. Some of those around the "fringe" gradually lost what little interest they had and left.

As time went by, scriptural knowledge of the church increased, and our experience with applying the new principles grew. I became more and more aware of the development of certain clearcut goals.

Unusual goals for me.

At other times in my ministry, I had set goals for the church, or someone else in higher echelons of church government had set them. They always centered around "nickels and noses." "Ten percent" seems to be a favorite among us ecclesiastical goal-setters. Ten percent gain in attendance, ten percent gain in membership, ten percent gain in offerings, and ten percent increase in the pastor's salary equals a "good year."

But the goals that were emerging in my mind now had almost nothing to do with the numbers and percentages. The new goals dealt instead with quality of church life. And they were based, not on a "success-mentality," but on New Testament priorities.

Lawrence O. Richards, in his book, *A New Face For The*

Church, has a significant section on goal-setting and development of a goal-oriented church program. [1] The *right* way is clearly to get the entire church involved in studying its scriptural purposes and working together to set its goals. Had I had Professor Richards' book two or three years earlier, I would have undoubtedly followed his advice and his outlines for doing this. But I was in a ministerial no-man's-land, and the Spirit had to work with who I was at the time.

I had founded the church and had trained it to follow me, implicitly impressing upon it the importance of my leadership. So it seemed natural to me (not knowing any better) to set *my own* goals and to present them to the church, not as an ultimatum or a "do-it-or-else" program, but as "information" about the direction I, as pastor, intended to lead the church. How fast we moved toward these goals was, of course, up to them. The congregation and its leaders in turn could veto the whole thing by terminating my call as pastor.

I see now that it's a rough-and-tumble way to go. But it was the only way I knew at the time.

These goals were presented to the organizational meeting of the church's leaders shortly after the church elections in late May. They are presented here, essentially as they were then. Were I writing them today, there would be only minor changes.

Goals for the Ideal Church

Family Focus: Every Christian family functioning as a unit for spiritual growth and spiritual sharing of life-in-Christ among family members. The Church not trying to do the family's job.

Scriptural basis: Deuteronomy 6:5-9

Spiritual Fellowship and Mutual Ministry to One Another: Fellowship on spiritual basis centered in Jesus, characterized by warm love between Christians, bearing of one another's burdens, mutual spiritual encouragement and concern, openness and honesty, mutual confession. A

[1] A *New Face for the Church* © 1970, (Zondervan Publishing House, Grand Rapids, Michigan) pages 187-208.

fellowship that actually strengthens faith in the reality of the Living Christ and results in spontaneous witness in the world.

Scriptural basis: Ephesians 4:11-16. 1 Corinthians 12, 13, 14; Romans 12:6-8; Hebrews 10:25.

Witness: The entire Christian community involved in day-to-day spontaneous sharing of Christ in their world of relatives, friends, business and social associates. Sharing that grows not from coercion or pressure of legalism, but that flows from hearts convinced of the reality of the Living Jesus by their mutual fellowship around Him and by services and preaching that builds disciples. Such sharing will show itself in the Christian's personal involvement in the lives of the people around him, so that, available to Christ, he has many *natural* opportunities to witness. This presupposes a church program that limits its demands on the Christian's time, so that he has time to permeate his personal world for Christ.

Scriptural basis: Matthew 28:19-20; Mark 16:15; Luke 24:44-48; John 20:21, 21:15-17; Acts 1:8, 2:1-47, 5:40-42, 8:1, 8:4, 8:26-39, 11:19-21; 1 Thessalonians 1:8.

Christian Service and Discipleship: Christians understanding that most important areas for Christian service are not within the organizational framework of the local church, but are found, as we yield to the Holy Spirit's leadership every moment of every day wherever we are and make ourselves available for involvement in the lives of people. Every Christian so in love with Jesus Christ that attendance at worship and CHUM groups, involvement in service, stewardship, witnessing and personal devotional life are simply a growing, careful expression of that love.

Scriptural basis: Matthew 22:37-39; Personal involvement of Jesus in the lives of others (Matthew, Mark, Luke, John); pattern of the early church in the Book of Acts; the "Sound-mind Principle" of 2 Timothy 1:7 and James 1:5.

Stewardship: Centers more and more, as time goes by, on concerns *outside* the local church: missions, pioneer churches, Christian education, aid to needy Christians, and evangelistic outreach in the community. Stewardship becomes more and more an act of love and faith and worship.

Scriptural basis: Matthew 6:33; Luke 6:38; Acts 11:27-30; 1 Corinthians 16:1-3; 2 Corinthians 8 and 9.

Outreach: Under the leadership of the Holy Spirit, the most important "steps of faith" the church takes are those involved in sacrificial, evangelistic outreach ministries: i.e., (1) beginning ("mothering") new churches, (2) use of mass media to spread the Gospel (newspapers, radio, television, billboards, etc.), (3) literature distribution, (4) underwriting evangelism among youth, college students, the aged, etc.

Scriptural basis: No specific basis for the specific programs suggested. Basis of "outreach concept": the Church in the Book of Acts.

Boards and Committees: Every business session of the church meets to bring glory to the name of Jesus. Primary concerns cease to be financial, physical, and official — but instead, the boards and committees are mainly concerned with the *spiritual life* of the Body and with fulfilling the Great Commission under the Holy Spirit's leadership.

Scriptural basis: Acts 2:41-47, 4:23-37, 6:1-8, 11:1-18 (an early church business meeting), 15:1-31 (settling a question of Church law); 1 Timothy, 2 Timothy, 1 Peter 5.

Physical Facilities: Simple-but-attractive, adequately furnished buildings large enough to house 1/4 to 1/5 of the total attendance expected. (For instance, with the addition of the new Sunday school building, Our Heritage should be able to handle 500 to 700 people by having four or five sessions of Sunday school and worship each Sunday.) [2]

Scriptural basis: The logic of good stewardship, based on James 1:5 and 2 Timothy 1:7.

Program: With the above goals and the New Testament pattern in mind:

(1) One large gathering of the congregation each week for edification and corporate worship.

(2) Every Christian involved in a small, more personal fellowship group each week.

(3) Special times of particular spiritual emphasis involving occasional overnight retreats, special periods involving several nights and days of Bible teaching or evangelism at the church, and certain service and social/fellowship events which are consistent with the purposes and needs of the Body of Christ.

(4) Business meetings and other activities, such as youth, women's musical, etc., deliberately kept at a needed minimum, to give families time to function as spiritual units and to give individuals time for witnessing/involvement with the people around them, and to give time for the Body to "permeate" its community for Christ.

Scriptural basis: (1) The mass evangelism and preaching of Jesus and the Apostles in Acts, in which they ministered to hundreds at once. Also: 1 Corinthians 16:2, Hebrews 10:25. (2) Ephesians 4:16; Acts 2: 46, 5:42. (3) Based on the ministry of Jesus and the apostles. (4) The logic of time and priorities: James 1:5 and 2 Timothy 1:7.

Pastor: Charged with the spiritual ministry suggested by the Apostles in Acts 6:4, "We will give ourselves to prayer,

[2] We have never built the proposed Sunday school building, but have exchanged facilities with the YWCA across the street and have two older classes which meet in homes. Furthermore, we feel the interests of the Kingdom can probably best be served through the proliferation of small congregations throughout the city, rather than trying to build one great "super-church."

and to the ministry of the Word." The pastor moves out of the position of Administrator-Evangelist-Organizer, as Spirit-led laymen, committed to New Testament ideals, realistically assume these responsibilities, allowing the pastor to devote his time to study, prayer, leading Bible study groups, giving spiritual counsel, and preaching/teaching the Word to individuals and the congregation.

Scriptural basis: Acts 6:4; 1 Peter 5; Ephesians 4:11-16; The ministry of Jesus and the apostles.

Less than a month after these goals were presented, clearly spotlighting the kind of church I felt the Spirit was leading us to become, eight church officers resigned and left the church with their families.

Here is part of one of the letters of resignation:

> This letter is written to inform you that we will no longer hold any office at Our Heritage Church.
>
> This is not a matter to be taken lightly nor is it so considered. After considerable discussion with our family and deep prayer with the Lord, we find that we cannot hold office in a church whose "goals" we find unacceptable. If these "goals" are the Lord's will, the staff of Our Heritage should devote itself completely to the fulfillment of this work. If the "goals" are not the Lord's will, then we want no part of them. In any event, after much prayerful consideration, we find that it is impossible to devote our efforts to that end.
>
> We will pray that the direction "Our Heritage" has chosen will prove to be the Lord's will and results in winning more people to Christ.
>
> Respectfully but sorrowfully . . .

I'm sure the quotes around the name of the church in the last paragraph were to emphasize the feeling that the writer considered the goals to be not goals of the *church*, but of the *pastor*. At the point at which this resignation came, that evaluation was probably largely correct.

But the scene is changing.

And, although I am sure the Lord Himself could have received more glory had men and women of differing opinions stayed and worked together in love, this "exodus of '69" cleared the way for nearly *sweeping acceptance* of these goals by the rest of the church. (Though that acceptance has never really been made "official" by vote of any authorized body. And it probably never will be.)

More and more you can ask the people of Our Heritage what their church is trying to do and you will get something similar to at least part of these goals. Not because they have memorized the goals themselves (many probably don't even remember that such a list of "goals" exists) but because they are participating in a church life of which some (not all) of these goals have become distinguishing *characteristics*.

These *"Goals for the Ideal Church"* are a part of membership training. They are reviewed once a year by the officers of the Church. They are distributed at times as an explanation of our fellowship. I go over them periodically to see if we are making progress toward what I believe to be something a little nearer "the Ideal Church" of the New Testament.

Perfection in any of these areas we have not attained. We have barely begun to move realistically toward some of them.

When Larry Richards suggested I write this story, my answer was, "Give us five more years. Then we'll look more like the renewed church. We've still too far to go, not enough to tell." He replied, "Write it *now*. It's needed *now*. You can write a sequel in five years if you want to."

So, while these are "goals" not yet fully realized – I'm writing. And though complete renewal is still out ahead somewhere, I am excited and rejoicing – for never in my ministry have I been so certain of my sense of direction.

It *feels* like renewal.

VIII

THE LETTER KILLETH BUT THE SPIRIT GIVETH LIFE

IF DETERMINING goals is important to finding church renewal, *how you go about reaching them is even more important.*

A congregation may set very spiritual goals for itself and still end up with only an empty, lifeless caricature of the living church they wanted to become, simply because they try to reach the goals through carnal (fleshly) means.

Real renewal can never be a work of the flesh. If it is, it isn't renewal. It's just re-dressing, re-organizing, re-structuring, or re-arranging – not renewal.

True renewal is a work of God. Man can never produce new life, no matter how hard he tries to "do it differently." The best he can do is temporarily to hide the death and decay of his own works behind some new facade of his own invention. But renewal ("revival," "newness") can only originate in the Living God.

This was the point of the Old Testament system embodied in *the Law*. The Law spotlights the utter inability of man to renew himself by his own efforts [1] – even though those efforts were directed toward *perfect goals.* [2]

After having demonstrated this fact for a couple of millenniums, God sent Jesus Christ, His Son, to terminate the old system, taking it to the cross with Him, [3] to make way for a *whole new*

[1] Romans 3:20, 8:3; Galatians 2:16, 3:11; Ephesians 2:8-9
[2] Romans 7:12-14
[3] Romans 7:4, Ephesians 2:15, Colossians 2:14

system.[4] Since the New Testament was written, man does not approach God or walk with God on the basis of his own performance or perfection, but on the basis of *Christ's* performance and perfection. "For we are not under the law but under grace" (Romans 6:14).

GETTING WITH THE NEW SYSTEM

The New Testament teaches that we not only *begin* fellowship with God by grace, but our entire relationship with Him and work for Him is carried on under grace, too.

In much of my preaching in the past, I have taught that the Holy Spirit, *by grace,* draws the sinner to Christ, because unregenerate man is utterly incapable of coming to Christ without the Spirit. I have preached that the Holy Spirit then renews that sinner, *by grace,* transforming him, regenerating, saving, cleansing, forgiving, re-creating him, and adopting him as God's child. This is the "new birth." At that moment, Christ comes to live in the man's heart. And if he were to die the next moment, he would go to heaven – "saved by grace."

But he doesn't go to heaven the next moment, so he must get to work doing things for God. Just as he threw all his energies into sinning and gratification of the flesh before, now he must throw all his energies, talents and faculties into doing all that God tells him in the Bible and through the church.

At this point, in my instruction of the believer, I would unconsciously move out of grace back under the law again! I taught him that, now that he was saved by grace, the man must, by self-discipline, work with all his strength to conform to the standard set by the New Testament and characterized in its highest sense by the effort to be completely "Christ-like."

So together, the believer and I, his pastor, began to try to whip the flesh into conformity with what we considered to be the Biblical image of the "spiritual Christian." We knew God would surely *help* the man. But, the man would have to do the work.

We believe we are saved by grace, because we know we cannot save ourselves. But, at the same time, we teach believers to per-

[4] Romans 7:6

form as Christians under the pressure of a system of "Christian law."

If Old Testament law shows up clearly the inability of man to reach God's perfect goals in human strength – New Testament law, which, in every case, *increases* the impossible height of the standard ("Be ye *perfect* as your Father in heaven is *perfect*"[5]) shows the weakness of the flesh even more vividly.

No one can live the perfect life of Christ, except *Christ.*

Now as a follower of Christ, the believer really wants to conform, obey and produce. He wants to cooperate with God and the church and with me, his pastor. So he allows me to press him into my mold. He conforms. He stops what I tell him to stop. He gets involved where I tell him he should get involved. He starts dutifully doing the Christian things.

And something in him begins to die!

We are surprised. "Where's the excitement and vibrancy and spontaneity he used to have when he was a new Christian?"

We shouldn't be surprised. Paul said it would happen. He said it as clearly as it needs to be said: "God . . . hath made us able ministers of the *new* testament not of the letter (of conformity to law), but of the Spirit: *for the letter killeth,* but the Spirit giveth life" (2 Corinthians 3:6, italics mine.)

The law, neither the Old Testament Law nor the *principle* of seeking to please God by conforming to an outward set of rules, could ever produce life. [6] The inevitable result of laying the law upon the flesh, trying to make human nature conform (even in a Christian), is always *death.* Frustration. Failure.

Renewal Is Life: Life Is the Spirit

The grace of God has not only provided new birth by the Holy Spirit. It has also provided new life in the Holy Spirit. [7]

No system of law can ever produce the life that pleases God. The weakness of sin-scarred human nature assures failure of any

[5] Matthew 5:48
[6] Galatians 3:21
[7] Romans 5:10

such set-up.[8] So, in Christ, at the cross, that old system was annulled. Laws and rules (even God's) aren't the issue any more under the new covenant.

> But now we are discharged from the Law and have terminated all intercourse with it, having died to what once restrained *and* held us captive. So now we serve not under (obedience to) the code of written regulations, but (under obedience to the promptings) of the Spirit in newness (of life)" (Romans 7:6, *Amplified New Testament*).

The new system under grace produces "newness of life" because it isn't based on a confrontation with cold commandments I can't obey – it is based, instead, on a living, personal *relationship* with the Holy Spirit, "The Spirit of *life* in Christ Jesus."[9]

The Spirit of Jesus living in me pleases the Father – completely. And the Spirit of Jesus living in me produces life. "Not I but Christ liveth in me."[10]

The Spirit puts God's laws into my heart and writes them in my mind.[11] The Spirit works in me both to will what pleases God and to do what pleases God.[12] The Spirit of God in me will do in and through me all God calls me to do.[13] The Spirit who began God's work in me will perform God's work in and through me until Christ comes again.[14] The Spirit who lives in me, since I trusted Jesus, fulfills all God's requirements by His presence in my life.[15]

Under the New Testament it's all different. It's not conformity, it's a relationship with a Person. It's not my failure, it's His success. It's not me working for God, it's God working through me. It's not service under the "oldness of the letter," it's service in "newness of the Spirit."[16] Not the letter but the Spirit. Not death but life. Not I but Christ. Not trying but trusting.

[8] Romans 7:18, 8:3, 8:8
[9] Romans 8:2 (italics mine)
[10] Galatians 2:20
[11] Hebrews 10:16
[12] Philippians 2:13
[13] 1 Thessalonians 5:24
[14] Philippians 1:6
[15] Romans 8:3
[16] Romans 7:6

This life in the Spirit, which fulfills God's goals for us, is released in us totally on the basis of faith. Trust. Dependence. It's a whole new ball game. And it cannot be played by the old rules.

When it comes to the matter of church renewal, the same principles apply. You cannot just intellectualize a new set of goals based on New Testament principles and then think you are going to reach them by the Old Testament approach.

The flesh cannot renew anything. You cannot get it to be spiritual or to do spiritual things. So there is no way you can legislate renewal. True renewal cannot be made to happen by manipulating people, nor by pressuring, condemning, coaxing, cajoling and educating people. Merely setting high goals and then striving for them will not do it.

There are no laws the church can establish which will make its people walk in the Spirit. Trying it is like trying to mix oil and water. They never really mix. The letter and Spirit are two different systems. They may appear to be mixed for a time, during the period of transition from law to grace, from life by the letter to life by the Spirit. (That's where we seem to be at Our Heritage. Dependence on ourselves and on man is so *natural*. So again and again we are discovered busily doing our own thing, laying the law on one another, measuring each other by some external human standard, rushing into action when waiting would be better. Impatient with the Spirit, we slip back under the law . . . and usually mess things up.) But while they may appear mixed to our finite eyes, in God's realm of spiritual absolutes the old system and the new cannot be mixed. The old was finished at the cross, the new began at Pentecost. The old is a piece of paper, the new is a Living Person. The old, because of human nature, always leads to death. The new, because of the Divine nature, always leads to life.

Life is the heart of all true church renewal. Renewal *is* life. And it can only come by the Spirit – never by the efforts of the flesh to renovate itself or its institutions.

"Not by (human) might, nor by (human) strength, but by my Spirit, saith the Lord . . ."[17]

As long as we operate the church or any of its agencies as institutions set up to teach the learners how to *act* like Christians, how to *conform* to the "acceptable evangelical norm," how to perform in the Christian manner, we shall not experience the fresh life we are seeking. Because we will still be "living under the law," intent on teaching the *flesh* how to look and act like it is living in the Spirit – even when that is not true.

(I am convinced that this is the thrust of much of what evangelicals are trying to do in Christian education – from pulpit to Sunday school class to Christian college campus.)

For true renewal, for spontaneous life in the Spirit to happen, preaching and teaching will have to move beyond the basic elements of the Gospel: the moral laws, the new birth, repentance, saving faith, baptism, the coming of the Holy Spirit, resurrection and judgment.[18]

Preaching on the new birth every Sunday has not kept our churches vital. The few uncommitted souls who happen to be in church are exposed to the elements of the Gospel, and a few of them have been renewed. But after that, they hear little to teach them how to go on with Christ. True, most are told to get baptised, to get busy, to begin witnessing, to pray, to read their Bibles and to join the church. But that's still elementary. Most will begin to do these things because they see them as good things to do. But these "good things," become an experience of *death* instead of life for multitudes of Christians, because they spring not from the life of the Spirit within, but from the same old human nature trying in the same old way to be good and to produce good works and to conform to an outside standard. It gets old and stale and dissatisfying and frustrating after a while – and unproductive. Because it's not from the Spirit at all. It's from the flesh.

Telling people over and over that they are born again doesn't

[17] Zechariah 4:6
[18] Hebrews 6:1-2

bring renewal. Preaching the super-performance standard of Jesus and the apostles doesn't do it.

The preaching of law (even "New Testament law"), getting people to ask "What would Jesus do?," carefully setting up the church organization and meeting structure and outreach pattern to conform to that of the New Testament church – none of these things will assure renewal.

Only when Christians and their churches learn (are taught) how to walk, in personal life and together in the Body of Christ, in utter dependence on the Holy Spirit, controlled by the Spirit, led by the Spirit, and in the energy of the Spirit, will we begin to touch the fringes of genuine life and renewal.

We think we have the Scriptures down pat. We know the law of God and the written and unwritten do's and don'ts of evangelicalism. From the Bible we can prove what is right and what is wrong. We can explain the doctrines that accompany our theological position. We know how to be orthodox. But *Life* (with a capital "L") eludes us. Because we have not yet caught the sweeping New Testament truth that *all of Christianity and all in the church and all in the Christian life functions rightly only in the context of personal relationship to, and control and empowerment by, the Living Holy Spirit.*

Just preaching the "doctrine" of the Holy Spirit has not brought lasting renewal, though it is a step in the right direction. There must also come a *practical* repudiation of the ability of the flesh to do anything apart from saturation and control by the Spirit.[19] And there must come a continual, actual, day-by-day, situation-by-situation turning from any dependence at all on the flesh to dependence completely and solely on the Spirit.

Our imperfect and limited experience with renewal started with this.

With us it started when the pastors began to repudiate their own ability to minister apart from the activity of the Spirit. We were driven to this position by sheer frustration, as I've already told you in the beginning chapters. Hemmed in by failure and

[19] John 15:5, Romans 7:18

the awful truth about ourselves and our church, under severe discipline from the Father, we were ready to listen when the truth came that, (1) it is impossible for us to do anything that counts without Jesus Christ, and (2) grace doesn't expect us to do anything without Him as the originator and doer of the work.

Almost immediately Carl and I experienced new freedom and rest. Jesus Christ, the Holy Spirit, became very real to us. We relaxed our feverish efforts in order to give the Spirit an opportunity to work. Free from the feeling that we had to produce for God if we expected Him to accept us, we falteringly took our first steps. The shackles of the old system released us the moment we decided simply to accept God's no-strings-attached love and grace and began to trust His Spirit instead of ourselves to obey the commandments, fulfill the commission, and produce works that please God.

Once we pastors saw it, we began to adjust our preaching and teaching to the truth the Spirit had revealed to us.

Before long, we, with our church, were beginning to touch the fringes of *Life*. The renewal we began to experience was real — a mere glimmer of what His best for us will involve, but nonetheless, the *real* glimmer of New Testament life in the Spirit.

Applying Grace-principles to Church Life and Christian Growth

How, if the renewal is to be a work of the Spirit and not merely a manipulation of the flesh, do you go about moving toward your New Testament goals? *How* do you assure that restructuring and reshaping is *real* spiritual progress toward renewal, not merely another performance by the flesh that eventually will take on the old taste of death?

I am sure God works with each of us exactly as we are. He knows what we know, what our hang-ups are, and how we will react to His leadership. He takes us right there — just as we are. And, that's where He wants to begin changing us and our churches. The way God moved to begin renewal in our fellowship and our lives may be different from the way He moves to renew you in yours. The Holy Spirit is a Person and He will act as a Person in the lives of each individual.

So what I'm sharing with you here is not meant to be a new system of *"renewal law."* This must not be viewed as a formula of ingredients which you mix together in the right proportions, stir, and suddenly your church is walking in the Spirit, living under grace.

This is merely the route the Spirit is taking us.

Christ Is Alive

First, as a leader, you stake your whole life and ministry on the fact that Jesus Christ is alive and that, in the Person of the Holy Spirit, He lives in you. He not only lives in you, He also lives in every true Christian believer. [20]

I Can Do Nothing

Second, you start admitting to yourself, honestly and deeply, that there is nothing that you can do all by yourself that could possibly be good enough to please God. You confess before God and it spills over into your public ministry that you realize that in you, in your human nature, there is "no good thing."[21] You openly and regularly face the fact that "without Christ you can do (absolutely) *nothing.*"[22] In other words, you accept the truth that, if it is to have any value at all before God, there is no part of your life you can live, and no part of your work you can do apart from the activity of God in and through you.

You are, yourself, completely dependent on God in and for everything.

Hanging Loose

Third, you throw yourself wholly upon the love and undeserved favor of God. Once you realize you are nothing and can do nothing without Him, there is nowhere else to go. You claim His forgiveness when you sin or fail. Your relationship with Him does not depend on your success — it depends on His grace and

[20] Colossians 1:27; 1 Corinthians 3:16; Romans 8:9.
[21] Romans 7:18.
[22] John 15:5.

forgiveness, so you can fail without being rendered utterly ineffective by the aftermath of guilt and self-condemnation. You are not under law, where everything depends on your performance — you are under grace, where everything depends on God.

When you start to see this with the eyes of faith, you will start to be able to relax, to rest, to "let go and let God." You will begin, by faith, to "hang loose."

The Dependent Life

Fourth, you seek to do everything you do, face every situation you face, by faith. You don't depend on yourself for anything. You don't depend on the people. You don't depend on your program, your training, your sermons, or your circumstances. You seek to depend completely on the Spirit.

You accept as a conviction the truth that "whatsoever is not of faith is sin,"[23] and that "the righteous live by faith."[24] So, you begin to look to God for everything. You don't count on anything or anyone but Him.

When you give a man a job to do — you depend on the Spirit to do it. When you preach — you depend on the Spirit to do it. When you pray or witness or plan or write or mow grass or eat breakfast or pick out your necktie or kiss your wife, you depend on the Spirit to do it.

You stop trying to do anything in order to let Him do everything. You make your heart, mind, lips, strength, and time available to Him. You act in faith and know, by faith, that the action is His. You speak in faith and you know, by faith, that the message is His.

Occasionally you take your life and the work into your own hands, depending, again, on yourself (you've slipped back under the law). You act, and you know the action is your own, and the result will be wood, hay, and stubble[25] . . . again.

When you wake up to what you've done, you admit it, and

[23] Romans 14:23
[24] Romans 1:17
[25] 1 Corinthians 3:12

know immediately it is forgiven, because you're not under law but under grace.

The New System at Work

Fifth, you teach these things to your congregation.

You dare to teach them the principle of grace, even though, humanly speaking, that is not nearly so "safe and secure" as teaching them the law. You start teaching them that they are free from the law, and that their relationship with Christ is not dependent on their performance but on His grace and forgiveness.

They may hang a little too loose for a while. For a time, they may sit down and look as if they are never going to do anything, while they are trying to find out how to rest in the Spirit and how to live under grace. They may try their new wings and test their new freedom.

You'll say to yourself, "Oh dear! I'd better lay down the law again. Things are getting out of hand."

But that is the road back to death and bondage.

So you decide, again, that the Spirit can be trusted and here's a chance for Him to prove it.

He always comes through. In "mysterious ways," He disciplines and chastens, corrects and reproves, and uses the members of His Body in a Spirit-led system of checks and balances.

And when the dust created by "kicking up their heels" settles, the freedom they have found in grace turns out to be freedom to follow the personal leadership of the Holy Spirit in practical ways that spell renewal and life for the church.

Or, if they were those who sat down and rested until you thought they were stuck in their spiritual rocking chairs: after they have learned to rest in the Spirit, they begin to move and work again, this time under His leadership and power. Even as they go to work, they are still at rest. And they have their priorities straight. The Spirit is doing it. It was worth the wait.

So you stop trying to "temper" the "risky" freedom of grace with the "safe" bondage of law. *You trust God to make His new system work.*

You talk more and more about the *Person* they now have living in them. Less and less about "thou shalt" and "thou shalt not." It's not that you ignore or evade the commandments. It is simply that you seek to show how the Holy Spirit within turns every commandment into a promise of life for the believer.

Biblical principles are preached and taught and studied in the groups. Practical applications of these principles are openly discussed. But the solution to any lack of conformity with these principles is not to impose the law or to draw hard lines of separation or condemnation, but to trust the Spirit to apply the truth as He wills, and to teach each believer to let the Spirit do in and through him whatever pleases God.

From the standpoint of those who feel they are "enlightened" on these matters, the instruction of the others must be done in the spirit of Matthew 7:1-5, Philippians 2:3, and Galatians 6:1, in full recognition that none of us is free from faults, we all have hang-ups and spiritual weaknesses we have not yet overcome. But God put us together to help each other up and over these things.

Our experience has been that the first issues dealt with by the Spirit are usually issues of faith, prayer, witnessing, attitudes, fellowship and love. In evangelical circles, the traditional approach is to deal with the easy external issues first. This is done by imposing pseudo-spiritual rules upon people to make them appear "spiritual" (which means acceptable to us) whether they are really spiritual inwardly or not. Most of the churches' efforts have been expended on dealing with secondary, peripheral things. Things that have little or nothing to do with the life of the inner man. Things that only tend to increase spiritual pride, conformity and bondage to "Christian law" . . . and a creeping, debilitating death in the church. [26]

If righteousness is by faith, as the New Testament says (Romans 1:17, Philippians 3:8-10, etc.), then, if a man will learn to *depend on the Spirit* of Christ, his life *will be righteous*. And that is what we must teach him first — all the while depending on the Spirit of Christ to teach Him through us.

[26] 2 Corinthians 3:6

The Spirit never speaks prematurely. He never exchanges one kind of bondage for another,[27] nor presses for an unnatural conformity to law.[28] *Men* do all these things. Sincerely. They just do not know any better. But, when the *Spirit* causes a man to live a holy life, it's beautiful. Spontaneous. A free, fresh, gushing artesian well of living water flowing "naturally" from inside the man.[29]

The church needs to learn to quit capping the well by the hard cover of imposed righteousness. The Spirit alone will make men holy.

The requirements of law are preached to children and to the unconverted. "The law," Paul says, "is our schoolmaster to bring us to Christ."[30] But to the saints (believers), the mechanics of grace and the freedom of life in the Spirit are taught.

Only under grace will the people of our churches ever launch out into the kind of personal lives of faith where they, alone with God, may experience His personal leadership, hear the voice of the Spirit speaking personally to them, and be led into and equipped for the kind of personal ministries that will make them really useful citizens in the Kingdom of God. Law stifles this. Grace opens the door to it.

The Minister Under Grace

Sixth, you don't just teach grace – you *apply* it daily in your ministry to those the Lord gives you. The key, of course, is to trust the Spirit of God instead of anything external or carnal.

While I fail at this many times and cannot claim anything near perfection in applying grace-principles to my ministry to people, here is some of what I've found a ministry under grace involves:

Accept people where they are. Do not expect perfection from them. Don't let your love and acceptance hinge on their performance as Christians.

[27] 2 Corinthians 3:17
[28] Galatians 5:18
[29] John 7:37-39
[30] Galatians 3:24

Forgive readily and as often as people fail. (You will want them to do this for you.) Live and teach the doctrines of mutual acceptance,[31] forgiveness,[32] *agape*-love,[33] no-condemnation,[34] bearing one another's burdens,[35] esteeming others better than one's self,[36] not judging or seeking to correct another apart from recognition of one's own failures and sins,[37] valuing highly the ministry of even the weakest believer.[38]

Resist the temptation to establish rules and to design "boxes" for people's spiritual lives. Resist the temptation to do the Holy Spirit's work for Him. Hands off! Let *Him* change them, remold them, reshape them, activate them. Get them to know Him and He'll do the work in them.

Encourage people to find their own ministry of life. Let them use their own ideas and make their own mistakes. Don't always protect them from embarrassment and failure. Allow time for them to personally seek, find, and obey the Spirit's leadership. Don't be so busy getting them busy that they can't go their own way following the Spirit, because they're too tied up going *your* way.

Practice waiting . . . waiting for God.

Waiting for God is basic faith. Waiting means refusing to do anything about anything in the flesh, refusing to depend on human ability, ingenuity or strength. It is trusting that God not only *can* do something about a situation but that He knows *when* to do it.

I'm the kind of guy who, when a need presents itself, a problem arises, a threatening situation develops, always wants to jump in with both feet and clear it up – *right now!* It's not that I'm heroic. I just can't stand to wait. I'm always convinced that there is something *I* can do in every situation – *right now.*

[31] Romans 14:1
[32] Matthew 6:14, 18:21-22
[33] 1 Corinthians 13
[34] Romans 8:1, Matthew 7:1
[35] Galatians 6:2
[36] Philippians 2:3
[37] Matthew 7:1-5, Galatians 6:1
[38] Romans 14:1, 1 Corinthians 12:22

After all, it is my duty as pastor to solve all problems and keep everything running smoothly. I'm driven by conscience and a sense of responsibility to do something – *right now.*

But the Spirit is teaching me that the solution to every exigency doesn't depend on me. He is completely dependable. He will show His own dependability and get all the glory, too, if I will repudiate my own efforts and "indispensability" and *wait for Him.*

He can get me involved if He wants to. And many times He does. But in situation after situation He has proved Himself adequate for the crisis without me.

Waiting is not only an act of faith, but again and again waiting has strengthened my faith and that of the church, as all of us watch God at work. And together we glorify Him for it.

". . . stand ye still, and see the salvation of the Lord."[39]

Since beginning to learn how to wait, we have seen Him work – singlehandedly – to get glory from predicaments involving false teachers, disruptive influences in the church, inter-personal problems, doctrinal differences, church finances, etc. We have seen Him alive, active and adequate for whatever it is – quite able to work His miracles without me always being in the middle of it, manipulating, protecting, guiding all affairs with my strong (?), *finite* hand.

The Focal Point

The focal point of this discussion of law and grace, the letter and the Spirit, the Old Testament and the New Testament, is to point up the reality of the Living Christ, and the fact that Christ alive and depended upon is the key to newness and life for the church and its members.

Christ is everything to renewal.

Renewal is something already provided by His life, death and resurrection – His grace. We need only to reach out *by faith* and take the newness He is.

By faith. By dependence on Him alone and completely.

Not by manipulation, clever strategy, or concerted human effort.

[39] 2 Chronicles 20:17

By faith in Him — faith that sees Him as real and alive and personally involved *today,* in the great work of renewing men and His Church.

If men of God can give up the notion that God's work is up to them, and will turn from depending on anything or anyone else, and trust only Him for all they need and for all it takes to reach the good goals He sets for His church, they will be renewed.

And their church will again be a church, a people . . . *alive!*

IX

A VEHICLE FOR THE SHARED LIFE

I WAS scared.

In the first place, I never did see myself as a teacher. But here I was heading for my very first "home Bible study group."

I did not do well in situations where spontaneous questions might be asked – where I would have to "think on my feet." So I had always made it a point to stay out of such situations wherever possible. (I even preach from a manuscript because I don't trust my spontaneous thoughts or my ability to express them coherently.) But here I was, walking into a situation where questions would be *sure* to be asked. And I couldn't possibly anticipate them all.

Although I thought of myself as an "evangelistic preacher," I always preferred to do my "evangelism" in a crowd that was at least somewhat sympathetic – like the average Sunday morning congregation or "revival" crowd (where Christians usually outnumber the "unsaved" about 99 to 1). But there I was, going into a home where I knew I would be talking informally with four couples, the theological leanings of which were a totally unknown quantity to me. When I arrived, I found one couple was Baptist, one Methodist, one Congregationalist and one Unitarian.

Only one of the group had invited Christ into his life. I'd led him to the Lord in the hospital. He had asked me to come to his home to meet with some of his friends and to lead them in Bible study.

I couldn't turn him down. After all, this is the kind of opportunity a pastor dreams about.

But as the day came, the thought of that varied group of unknown people became a threat to my image of adequacy – and I faced it with trepidation.

We had decided to use Campus Crusade's Bible study booklet, *The Uniqueness of Jesus.* My plan was to play the recording of Dr. Bill Bright's message on the subject and then to discuss it. The album jacket suggested several questions to guide the discussion:

1. In what way is Jesus of Nazareth the unique personality of all time?
2. Define sin.
3. What are the ultimate consequences of sin in the life of man?
4. What provision has God made to pardon sin?
5. What must man do to receive pardon from sin?
6. What can Jesus of Nazareth do for man that no one else can do?
7. What reasons do men have for rejecting Christ?
8. What is involved in becoming a Christian? [1]

I spent three hours preparing my answers to these very basic questions.

The beginning went smoothly. Coffee was served. Ashtrays were in use, and the air was full of smoke as a friendly and interested group of eight men and women relaxed to listen.

I explained that the purpose of the group was to see what the Bible says about Jesus Christ so that we could get to know Him better. I assured them that I was not there to proselyte or to grind my little denominational ax, but simply to learn *with* them.

I distributed the Bible study booklets, collected a dollar from each couple to pay for them, distributed the Bibles I had brought, and turned on the hi-fi.

[1] From the record jacket of "*The Uniqueness of Jesus,*" available from Campus Crusade for Christ, Arrowhead Springs, San Bernardino, Calif.

From that point on, nothing I had so carefully planned went as I had so carefully planned it.

Within seconds after the discussion began, my carefully planned notes containing "all the answers" became something for my nervous fingers to fumble. More was needed than "pat" answers supported by a few proof texts.

The discussion moved away rapidly from the nice, safe questions on the album jacket. I found myself involved in discussing subjects for which I had not prepared at all. Is sin even real? Why do you accept the Bible's authority without question? Is it really necessary to believe that Jesus is God? Why do you believe He is God? Because the Bible says so? Why should I accept that?

These were well-educated, well-read, intelligent, aware people. They were not antagonistic. They simply were not afraid to ask questions.

When the two-hour session ended, they unanimously wanted to meet again in two weeks to go on with the study.

I hadn't been totally without answers. But as I walked out with my unused notes tucked neatly in my much-used Bible, I felt like a total failure. I felt that the study had completely gotten away from me! It seemed I had not led the group at all – they had led me! It had gotten completely out of my control!

But in the next couple of days, as my wounded ego began to heal, I realized that something very exciting and significant had taken place. While I was all hot and bothered about losing control of the meeting and about not having been shown up too well as a teacher, the group – this group of modern pagans – had been *learning*. They had taught each other. And they had taught *me*. They had exposed their true feelings. For the first time they had been in the Word of God in serious quest for answers for their lives. They had faced some spiritual realities. They had, in some cases, gotten off the fence on spiritual issues they had been ignoring. The relevance for their lives of certain spiritual truths had begun to come through. For the first time in most of their lives, Christ was an issue, the Bible was speaking, and sin was being discussed.

God had set me and my carefully prepared presentation aside to show what *He* can do with a small group in His Word.

As I prepared for the second confrontation with the group, I spent only about an hour, and much of that time just saying, "All right, Holy Spirit, You alone know what's going to happen tonight. I'm just going to trust You."

By the end of the first six sessions some very significant changes had taken place. The group was now going from house-to-house for their meetings, which now lasted two and a half to three hours. The sharing was real and honest. At least four had committed their lives to Christ. All had become more active in their own churches, or had begun attending ours. And even the Unitarian couple was calling Jesus "the Son of God"!

And I was sold on small groups for evangelism and on the Holy Spirit's ability to do His work with a minimum of help from me!

This experiment took place about a year before the ideas of Larry Richards and Watchman Nee, described in Chapters 3 and 4, came to me.

The encouragement to try it came from the combined influence of Keith Miller's *A Taste of New Wine,* [2] an introduction to Campus Crusade's "Action Groups," [3] and one enthusiastic new believer who wanted his friends to hear what I had told him about Jesus.

At first, I saw it only as a very effective tool for evangelism. But God was also using this first exciting group to teach me some unforgettable lessons about His Body.

A year later, I was shown the church as the Scriptures reveal it. I looked in dismay at the church as I knew it and realized how little similarity there was between it and the Scriptural church. When the suggestion came that small groups might be part of the answer for returning the church to its New Testa-

[2] Word Books, Waco, Texas

[3] Especially helpful was *The Teachers' Manual for the Ten Basic Steps to Christian Maturity,* Dr. William R. Bright, Campus Crusade for Christ, Arrowhead Springs, San Bernardino, California.

ment life-style, I was totally receptive. I had been in an effective small group. I had seen how the Spirit used it.

The Body of Christ (the church of the Scriptures) is a *unique spiritual body* put together and given its oneness by the Living Spirit of Jesus who lives in and ministers through each member for the edification of all.[4] The living church is *a priesthood* of men and women to whom is committed the ministry of life to one another, having been given by the Spirit all the "gifts" (equipment) necessary to carry on this priestly ministry.[5] The church of the New Testament is *a caring fellowship* bound together by a single faith and by love.[6] The real church is a fellowship of people capable of helping, encouraging, instructing, rebuking, warning, and guiding one another.[7]

The life of the church as the New Testament describes it, in such passages as 1 Corinthians 12 and Ephesians 4:1-16, is the life of a *body*. Every cell is dependent on every other cell. Every organ relies on the functioning of every other organ. None lives to himself. All live for and from the others. If one suffers all suffer. The whole is edified by the proper ministry of every part. The church's life is not many individual lives put together in an organization. The church has only *One Life*. And all its members share that *One Life* in common.

The One Life all share in common, the One Life each ministers to the others, is the Life of Jesus Christ – the Life of the Holy Spirit.

The living church is *a body whose very life is Jesus Christ*. He is personal to them. He lives in them and they know it. He is real to them. Alive to them. Working in their lives. And He comes to them in living ministry through other members of the Body in whom He dwells. That makes the Body indispensable to one's personal spiritual well-being and communication with Christ.

As I have already said . . . I scanned the church I was pastoring

[4] Ephesians 4:1-16
[5] 1 Corinthians 12, 13, 14
[6] Ephesians 4:1-6
[7] Hebrews 10:25

for traces of the two-thousand-year-old priesthood of believers. But the instances in which I found it functioning were the exceptions, not the rule. A Sunday school teacher here, a singer there, the pastor from his pulpit, the rare, nearly accidental development of deep fellowship between two or three families (and we tended to think of them, negatively, as a clique).

"Why?" I queried. "Why is the priestly ministry, the flow of life between cells an exception rather than a general characteristic of church life?"

The answer echoed back from the word pictures of the church in century one: "Because there is no opportunity in your church for such ministry. You don't really believe in it. And you are, by the very structure of your church, its meetings and its program, keeping such a caring, mutually helpful ministry between members from happening!"

Then Larry Richards' articles[8] suggested that the church set less important things aside and fill this vacuum with opportunity in the form of small groups he dubbed "growth cells."

Professor Richards, Keith Miller, Bill Bright and others like them were certainly not the first men in history to recognize that a return to small groups of believers ministering to each other could be a spark to ignite the flame of renewal in the church. The truth is, that nearly every major spiritual awakening in the last two thousand years was accompanied, spontaneously or by design, by the huddling of tiny cells of Christians, away from the institutional church, to study the Bible, pray, and minister to one another.

In fact, these modern men named above, cannot be said, in any sense, to be the originators of the so-called "small group movement" today. The Holy Spirit is the originator. Spontaneously, in many parts of the world at once, people, hungry for more than they were getting from the established churches (liberal and conservative), began to gather in homes, offices, dormitories and factories — across denominational lines — to find spiritual reality and to pray together.

[8] *A New Face for the Church,* Zondervan.

Some church leaders have blindly opposed this movement. Evidently, they are quite ignorant of the historical fact that almost every widespread revival has been accompanied by this phenomenon. Such opposition itself is according to history. Every small group movement in Christian history, including the first such movement, has been opposed by the established religious leadership.

The details of that one are chronicled in the New Testament.

> And all that believed were together, and had all things common; and sold their possessions and goods, and parted them to all men, as every man had need.
> And they, continuing daily with one accord in the temple, and breaking bread *from house to house,* did eat their meat with gladness and singleness of heart, praising God, and having favor with all the people. And the Lord added to the church daily such as should be saved.
> And daily in the temple, and *in every house,* they ceased not to teach and to preach Jesus Christ (Acts 2:44-47, 5:42, italics mine).

There were no Christian churches built until after A.D. 300, though archeological diggings have uncovered a couple of houses in Rome dating to the late second century. These had been modified for meeting places by removing the inside walls. The relics found in these houses indicate the possibility that these had been places for Christians to assemble.

Jewish Christians maintained their faithfulness to temple worship until they were excommunicated for their faith in Christ. Before persecution halted them, Christian gatherings, such as those described in Acts 2:46 and 5:12, were held in the temple in Jerusalem. But even before persecution and excommunication, from the earliest record of church life in Acts 2, believers not only assembled for large apostolic teaching sessions, but for small, informal, house-to-house "soul-fellowship" sessions.

As the heat of Jewish and then Roman persecutions increased, a regular schedule of mass meetings became too risky, so the "church-in-the-home" became *the focal point* of the church's life and of its teaching and its mutually edifying "Body ministry."

Other references to these home churches are found in Acts 12:

12, 16:40, 28:23, 30-31; Romans 16:5, 23; 1 Corinthians 16:19; Colossians 4:15 and Philemon 2.

The New Testament indicates that these little churches were not only a practical necessity, because of the absence of Christian buildings and the persistence of persecution. But even (according to those early references in Acts) before persecutions started and while the temple was still available, they were part of the Spirit's plan for a living Body which thrives on *Koinonia* – soul-fellowship.

The demise and re-emergence of small Christian home meetings has continued from century one to the present.

In the years preceding the Reformation, *before* Martin Luther nailed his "Ninety-five Theses" to the door of the church at Wittenburg, small, unrecognized, unblessed groups of searchers were meeting away from the established church to study the Bible and to pray. The Spirit was already tilling the ground in preparation for the Protestant Reformation based on the Word of God.

Someone said, "Methodism began to lose its fire when it built its first church building."

History records that the flames of the revival that saved England from a bloodbath such as the French Revolution, were fanned and kept hot, not only by the great preaching of men like John Wesley and George Whitfield, but by one of the "methods" that gave the movement its name. That "method" was a *small group movement* known as the "class meeting."

Twelve believers comprised a "class." They met regularly to encourage, exhort and instruct one another in the Christian life. They cared for each other, prayed for each other, and were open and frank with each other.

When Wesley discovered that one of his preachers was neglecting to get the members of his "Methodist Society" (church) involved in class meeting life, he would reprimand the man firmly and instruct him to divide his society into classes of twelve. Then, to lead these classes, the pastor was to select the *weakest* member of the group and appoint him to lead. The result must have been that, with a weaker Christian as leader, all members of the group became more involved in mutual ministry. And the priesthood of believers functioned.

The "great revivals" of American history were nearly always preceded and followed by small groups meeting for prayer and personal renewal.

Many Christians believe that the spontaneous "small group movement" which has been gaining momentum, mainly among laymen, for the past decade or so is part of the preparation for what will be the greatest spiritual awakening the world has ever known since Pentecost. If that's true, the institutional church had better wake up to it and bless it and *become part of it,* or what God is doing in this generation may pass that old wineskin by. And when the "new Pentecost" comes, the established church could be on the outside looking in!

It is clear, then, that we were doing nothing new, when, in our search for some way to let the church function as the Body of Christ, we chose small groups as our chief *modus operandi.* They seemed to us to be the nearest thing we had seen to the kind of natural setting where the life of the church could become "The *Shared* Life." They seemed the kind of church structure which would allow the Holy Spirit the most freedom to do what He wanted to do in and through the Body.

X

LIFE IN THE LITTLE CHURCHES

THEY ARE called "The Little Churches." This is to make it clear that the small home groups in which the people of Our Heritage Church are involved are not "agencies" of the church or another form of "auxiliary" – they *are* the church.

At first, we followed Professor Richards' suggestion and called them "Growth Cells."

Later, Carl suggested a meaningful acrostic, and for two years the groups were called "CHUM Groups." C-H-U-M: "Christian Home Unit Meetings."

But our conviction grew that these groups should see themselves not only as *part* of the Body of Christ (which they certainly are), but as microcosms of the greater Body. We came to believe that they were *in fact* the living Body of Christ in operation. The small group, as we envision it, and have experienced it, *is the church.* (This does not mean, in any sense, that the whole congregation of Our Heritage is any less "the church" than it was before. If anything, it functions even more as the Body of Christ than it ever did before.)

That is why we have chosen to refer to them as "The Little Churches." We want them to realize what they are. We want them to know that whatever they find the New Testament saying to the church applies not only to their "mother church," or to the universal church, but to their "Little Church."

We do not try to obtain conformity in this. Ask members of these groups about the one in which they are involved, and they may refer to theirs as "the Bible study group," "CHUM Group," "Bible Rap," "our group," or . . . "The Little Churches."

Fear was no stranger to us as we made plans to change the whole structure of the church, to begin building it around small groups. When one has been trained in the pastor-centered approach to church life almost from birth, the idea of turning "*my* people" loose in small groups without the "benefit" of strong pastoral guidance was a little terrifying.

I was afraid we would wind up with a divided church – many little cliques all going their own way. A few strong lay leaders would begin to exert more influence over the church than the pastor, I feared.

I was afraid that, free from my control and teaching, some groups would get off into false doctrines or doctrines contrary to those acceptable to my denomination. False teachers might get in and run off with part of my flock.

Without me to keep things on course, I imagined, some groups might get off the Word and into certain legalistic or psychological excesses. I had read stories and editorials about "sensitivity training" and certain way-out group therapy experiments. One pastor-friend was not impressed at all when he heard about our groups. The image he had of the "small group movement" was gained from wild stories circulating through his denomination's "grapevine" about some evangelist in California who got the members of his groups to be "open" with one another by taking off their shoes and sitting in a close circle, touching their bare toes together!

Yes, I had fears. And my fears received strengthening help from respected pastor friends who warned me against the direction we were about to take.

But I had also received a new "revelation" of the Body of Christ. And I had to answer two persistent questions:

(1) Am I satisfied with the church as it is today?

(2) Can the Holy Spirit be trusted?

The answer to the question made me willing to go ahead, in spite of my fears. The fact is, that when one places confidence in the complete adequacy of the Spirit, fear is turned into anticipation — eager looking forward to seeing just how He will work. Problems are reborn as adventures.

A Lay Institute for Evangelism was to be conducted by Campus Crusade for Christ at Our Heritage Church the weekend before Thanksgiving. *Providentially* it had been put on the calendar several months before the revolution in our thinking about the church began to happen.

We now saw this event as a "natural" for launching the development of the first "little churches." Elvis Priest, Arizona Lay Division Director, was asked to incorporate into his basic plan of Lay Institute training, an emphasis on "Action Group Strategy." The concept of the "Action Group" was stated in material from the organization's Lay Division Office:

> The action group concept consists of a strategy for building Christian disciples. A small group of Christians within a church are bound together by their faith in Christ and by a desire to meet regularly to encourage one another in seeking to help fulfill the Great Commission of Christ (Matthew 28:10-20).[9]

The purpose of Crusade's "Action Groups" was close to what we envisioned at that time for the groups around which we planned to structure the church:

> A. To provide small, vital group fellowship as was common in the early church.
> B. To provide opportunities for mutual encouragement and growth through the discussion and sharing of the Word of God.
> C. To provide an opportunity for small group prayer.
> D. To train and encourage church members in personal evangelism.
> E. To provide a means to channel new converts into membership and active participation in the local church.
> F. To build disciples capable of planning and implementing a strategy for evangelism outreach through the local church.[10]

At the close of the Lay Institute for Evangelism, we announced the formation of two "growth cells." One group would start the

[9] Lay Institute for Evangelism, *Action Group Strategy*, Campus Crusade for Christ, Arrowhead Springs, San Bernardino, California.

[10] Ibid.

week following the institute, the second would begin a week later. Both would run on an "experimental basis" for six weeks, at the close of which the group itself would decide whether or not to continue.

The pastors arbitrarily divided the lay institute attenders into two groups (geographically) and then telephoned each one to invite him or her to his assigned group. Spouses were invited too, whether they had received the training or not – whether they were believers or not.

Carl took temporary leadership of one group, and I the other. We had no definite plan as to when that leadership would pass to the group itself. We would depend on the Spirit to lead. As it turned out, it was necessary for Carl to stay with his group for nearly a year. It was only two weeks until the leadership of the other group began to be passed weekly from member to member.

Each group, we were learning, has a personality of its own. Trying to put every group into the same pigeon hole, may stifle its uniqueness and freedom to follow the Spirit's plan to meet the peculiar needs of the people in each individual group.

Both groups were started with the Bible study booklet, *The Uniqueness of Jesus,* [11] by William R. Bright. In fact, we used that booklet as a "starter" for nearly all of the groups begun during the first two years. Each group member paid for his own copy.

The midweek service (which was nothing but a small group anyway) was dropped so that it would not detract from something we expected to be far more valuable and important. By the time the first "little churches" began, we pastors were involved in a concerted effort to weed out many of the committee meetings, "busy work" assignments, and social gatherings from the church calendar to make certain that secondary things would not be a legitimate excuse for non-involvement in the vital new happening.

A living room full of people awaited my arrival that first night – the night before Thanksgiving. Ashtrays were provided for those who wished to smoke. I carried a supply of study booklets, Bibles for those who did not bring their own, and pencils.

[11] Campus Crusade for Christ, Arrowhead Springs, San Bernardino, Calif.

First, we had the rather shallow introductions with which we usually satisfy ourselves: "State your name and where you work." Then, after a brief opening prayer, I distributed a yellow mimeographed sheet designed to elucidate the purpose and procedures of the new "growth cell."

GROWTH CELLS

Purpose

To get to know Jesus Christ better . . . To learn to share Him with one another, our families at home, and our world . . . To develop a deep awareness of the Body of Christ.

The Growth Cell Meeting

Sharing Experiences in Christ

Joys, failures, discoveries, problems, witnessing experiences, and things that happen as we take Christ through the routine of daily life.

Sharing Bible Study

Every Growth Cell member prepares in advance. All share insights, questions, doubts, and personal applications ("How the Lord has spoken to me through this passage").

Sharing Strategy for Touching Our World for Christ

Training, discussion, and planning for effective witnessing through Growth Cell, family and personal contacts.

Sharing Prayer

Conversational prayer [12] growing out of the sharing of experiences, Bible study and strategy.

[12] Group conversational prayer is different from the "traditional prayer meeting prayer" in that it is approached as a *conversation with* God, not an *address to* Him. It involves "just talking" to God, using sentence prayers, covering one subject at a time, and bringing up prayer requests as you pray. In conversational prayer, a participant may pray more than once, just as in a conversation you probably will speak more than once. It helps "conversation with God" to be able to use the conventional term "You" when speaking with Him, instead of the Old English "Thee" or "Thou." Suggested book: *Prayer: Conversing With God* by Rosalind Rinker, published by Zondervan.

Individual Responsibility

1. Prepare for the Bible Study.
2. Pray daily for each member for the Growth Cell.
3. Witness regularly.
4. Work for the growth and witness of each member of your own family.

Again, the *experimental* nature of this group was stressed. In six weeks the group would end, unless *they* wanted it to continue.

At the beginning, our hope was that the "little churches" involve *all members of the family* from the seventh grade up. We could not imagine the early church doing it any other way. All age groups met together.

Of the two "pioneer" groups, one immediately rejected the idea of having their children present, feeling that it would inhibit freedom to discuss family problems. The other group decided to try the family approach. And for the first four or five meetings, children and teenagers were present.

It was not successful. The church has been splintering age groups for so long that we did not know how to make it work. The conversation by-passed the children most of the time. The teenagers felt outnumbered and soon dropped out. I felt they added something the group needed, but there was seldom anything discussed that related specifically to their problems, so it was inevitable that the group become an adult meeting.

After three years, we are once again seeking to bring Christian teenagers, who wish to be involved, into little churches with adults. I am optimistic about the results. I feel we are now ready to bridge the gap in the dimension of the Spirit.

We were not disappointed with those early group experiences. Almost immediately, the spiritual growth we had been unable to produce through church services and preaching became visible. And it was clear that we had produced none of it. The Spirit, ministering through His believer-priests, was producing growth that was spontaneous and real.

After just three meetings of these two groups, I was asked to speak to a group of pastors, and I shared with them what was happening:

All my sermons on evangelism have not awakened Christians to their responsibility and the power available *in them,* in the Holy Spirit, to do witnessing and to live with Christ constantly, as just *one* of these experimental "growth cells" has.

In three weeks of its operation, one man who has rejected Christ for years has come to Christ and is sharing life with the group . . .

Another man, a brand new, timid Christian has been given courage to share Christ with his boss . . .

His wife asked the group's help in straightening out her bad attitudes so that her witness to her sister would be effective . . .

A home on the verge of a break (we were only faintly aware of this before the group started meeting) has begun to mend. The wife, a vacillating, defeated, sinning Christian for years, has discovered the power of the Holy Spirit for her temper and her problems at home. Her unconverted husband, quite "anti-Christian" before, has begun to *come with her* to the meetings . . .

A teenager involved in the group asked the group to pray for her as she spent the weekend with a Buddhist exchange student to whom she would be witnessing . . .

The girl's mother asked for advice and prayer as she tries to share Christ with a dying Jewish girl . . .

A United Fund executive shared how he'd prayed for fifteen minutes with an alcoholic who came to one of the United Fund agencies in desperation . . .

Tonight, the group's leader is bringing with him to the "growth cell" a man who has been a confessed "atheist" for years . . . A man the group leader led to Christ last Sunday!

The group has grown so fast that after three weeks we are considering dividing it. Last week, of fifteen people present, seven shared witnessing experiences from their week.

The Holy Spirit is reviving our church. Our people are learning to share the life of Christ together and to apply Him to everyday needs. A new "Body-consciousness," a new mutual concern for one another in Christ, and a new concern for their world is taking shape at Our Heritage. And, around these Christian families, who have discovered the reality of Christ, *the world is changing* . . .

Christ is changing the world through His Body.

Though the sense of excitement over what we could see God doing was over-shadowing and minimizing our problems, there were some imperfections and hang-ups that needed working through in those early groups.

Any person or group who has a wonderfully beneficial experience with the Lord, unless they are carefully instructed otherwise, has a tendency to "generalize" their experience. "Everyone needs this," is the first reaction. Then, human pride (flowing from the deceitful heart of man[13]) almost invariably adds (though probably not nearly so overtly as this), "And those who don't take advantage of this experience are *less spiritual than we are!*" Thus rises the ominous spectre of spiritual pride, self-righteousness and condemnation of others. It is a favorite and effective device of the satanic enemy to pollute and spoil even the good things God does for us.

This is one of those "hang-ups" of which I spoke above. And there were others.

I thank God for a wise pastoral colleague named Vince Strigas. Not with the intention of discouraging what we were trying to do, but out of genuine concern that we avoid some of the pitfalls into which some groups fall, Vince took me aside, bought me a coke, and shared some of his insights. The seeds of some of the problems he pointed up were already sprouting in our exciting new "cells."

After my conversation with this friend, I headed for my mimeograph again. Pulling together Vince's counsel and some additional thoughts from brief experience in the "little churches," I "published" a sheet designed to head off potential problems before they became problems. Here it is:

ADDITIONAL NOTES ON GROWTH CELL LIFE

1. *It is Jesus Christ who can meet our needs.* The Growth Cell is only a means of getting to know Him better with the help of other believers. It is not the end in itself. If the group fails to bring us to Him every week, it has truly failed.
2. *We discover Christ in the Bible.* Our experience with Him must always be in keeping with His Word. Bible study is therefore the *most important part* of the Growth Cell meeting.

[13] Jeremiah 17:9

3. *Growth Cell sharing of experiences must not be confession of sins.*[14] Confess every known sin to *Christ.* He alone can forgive and cleanse (1 John 1:9). If a problem is of an extremely personal nature, but help is needed, share it privately with another Christian, or request prayer in a general manner.
4. *Beware of boasting.* Rather, "This is what Christ has done."
5. *Growth Cell sharing of witnessing experiences must not lead to legalism.* Never seek to create "pressure" to witness. Never let the idea slip into the meetings that everyone *must* report so many people witnessed to. *If* you've had a good witnessing experience, share it. Share witnessing problems about which the group can give advice and pray. Remember, witnessing must be backed by *living.*
6. *Beware of domination of the meetings by any one person.*
7. *Leaders must keep the group on target with the purpose,* and bring it back if it begins to stray from that purpose.
8. *Be careful of developing a "Pharisee attitude."* The group must never reflect the idea that "we are more

[14] Were I preparing this list today, I probably would not include this caution. At the time, I feared that the openness and honesty that we were encouraging might cause sharing of problems to degenerate to the unhealthy level where confession of sins became the "in" thing to do. I had heard of groups where this happened. As a result, members of the group, caught in the desire to be "in" and to gain special attention would try to confess more sin or a "worse" sin than others – even if they had to *make up something* to confess.

This has never been a problem with any of our groups. Instead, there has been a most desirable openness and honesty, in which, as the group shares in study of the Word together, sins and faults and weaknesses are freely confessed. The group discusses these problems, applies the light of the Word to them, prays together over them. They help the one overtaken in a fault or sin to bear the burden. They intercede for one another in these matters during the week. Then, as healing comes, they rejoice together. And through the whole process a deep bond of love develops within the group.

It is a good thing to follow James' instructions, "Confess to one another your faults – your slips, your false steps, your offenses, your sins; and pray also for one another, that you may be healed and restored – to a spiritual tone of mind and heart" (James 5:16, *Amplified* New Testament).

spiritual because we are in a Growth Cell." *Judge not* (Matthew 7:1-5). *Adopt the attitude:* "We have no idea why anyone is not here (they may have good reasons), but we *do* know why *we* are here – to meet Christ for *our needs.* I cannot change anyone else's life, but Christ can change *mine,* and I want that!"

9. *Invite and encourage, but never pressure, argue or try to force anyone into the Growth Cell.* Let the Holy Spirit do it, if He wants them there.
10. *When meeting with the congregation, remember that you are one with the whole Body of Christ, not just the Growth Cell.*

When the group begins to catch the concept of walking in the Spirit and sharing group life under grace instead of under law,[15] such a sheet of cautions becomes superfluous. No rules are needed. The Spirit ministering through His Living Body and the Word takes care of all these "problems."

If the group fails to catch the concept of life in dependence on the Spirit, no set of rules can ever get it through its crippling hang-ups.

As life in the little churches has evolved from that beginning, it has become much less formal and the parts of the meeting have become much less distinct from one another. All the elements we wanted are still there. But now they all seem to run together, with Bible study and conversational prayer as the central activities. Sharing of experiences and emphasis on witnessing (not "training" or "strategy" as our original ideas called for, but Spirit-motivated reporting, discussion of the "how-to's" and encouragement), flow together into a weekly experience of fellowship around Jesus, in which what happens all seems quite "natural." There is a free spirit that allows for meaningful sidetracking into areas of group and individual concern and need.

The amount of time people spend together each week is up to them. The meetings vary in length from thirty minutes (dur-

[15] See Chapter 8

ing lunch hour on high school campus) to three or four hours (in some of the adult groups). Most of the groups share refreshments together, though in our original planning we intended to discourage this. In addition to regular meeting time, the group occasionally plans a picnic or some other extra fellowship event. Occasionally, two or more groups will combine to hear a speaker, or to share pot-luck.

Before they have met together very long, the group becomes more than just a weekly meeting. Deep friendships develop. The telephone lines bring between-meeting prayer requests. There is someone to go to with problems and with whom to share good news. The week-between may involve dinner with another couple from the group. Two or three of the ladies may get together for coffee, conversation and/or prayer. A golf game, or two men getting together for a lawn mower repair project turns into another session of sharing what the Lord is doing. A casual visit becomes an opportunity for a conversation-in-depth about a problem mentioned at the last group meeting.

Caring. Bearing one another's burdens. Intercession. The development of the kind of love by which all men will know that we are His disciples. [16]

I can't love a thousand people like that. I can't love even a hundred like that. But I can love ten people. My experience with Spirit-produced *agape*-love can begin to be real there . . . in a small group.

It must eventually go farther than that, of course. But the little church can, at last, give me a place to *start loving.*

Multiformity

Geography or locality is probably the most Biblical basis for deciding who should become involved in a particular group. Our first two little churches were formed with geography as at least one factor in their formation. But since then, other criteria have seemed more pressing.

[16] John 13:34-35

Our first two groups were essentially adult groups (both single and married). And the formation of adult groups, with an emphasis on married couples, has been the direction of our greatest concentration, ever since groups became "the program of the church."

But some of our most fruitful and exciting little churches have been groups of women, meeting during the day. Our largest group is the teenage "Bible Rap," which meets initially as a large group (forty to fifty teens and collegians), and then splits into small groups which meet for sharing and prayer in three or four different areas of the house. Two men's groups meet for breakfast, Bible study and prayer each week. There is also a home group for junior high students. Several small groups of students meet on local high school campuses.

Other suggestions as to group make-up include groups for younger adults and groups for older. Or groups for parents with children about the same age. Collegians' groups (Collegians at Our Heritage are mixed with teens or adults, according to their own choice). Groups for alcoholics. Groups for new Christians. Evangelistic groups for non-Christians.

All have advantages. All have unique ministries they can perform. All should be operating somewhere.

However, the little church which is a true microcosm of the greater Body of Christ is the one which involves all age groups, all levels of spiritual maturity, all types of life-situations, both sexes, married and single and divorced, all economic levels, and, if the neighborhood is mixed, both black and white. Obviously, not many groups will be all these things. Size alone will limit them. But by maintaining a somewhat "general" character, they can function in the fullest sense as the church, leaving their make-up to the wisdom and work of the Holy Spirit.

Evangelistic Bible Study Groups

Probably the most exciting way a little church can be started, is for one or two Christian couples (or, one or two Christian women, men, or young people) to invite a group of their neighbors and friends who are not Christians into their home for Bible study.[17]

They are clearly told that the purpose of the gathering is to study the Bible. Discussion centers on the very basic elements of the Gospel. A verse-by-verse study of *First John* or *The Gospel of John* is a good place to start. Or a Bible study booklet, such as Campus Crusade's *The Uniqueness of Jesus,* is used. (Other sources of such materials include the *Navigators,*[18] and the *World Home Bible League.*[19]

Gloria came to Our Heritage and discovered new life in Christ. Family circumstances made it impossible for her to become a member of the church, and shortly after she came to know Christ she even had to stop attending. One day she called me and asked if I would be willing to meet with a group of her friends if she could get them together to study the Bible.

The time was set, and on a weekday morning I went to one of her friends' homes, where Gloria had gathered a group of ten housewives representing five or six denominations. None were in any way connected with Our Heritage. Most were from non-evangelical congregations. Most did not know Christ in a personal way.

I started with them in *The Uniqueness of Jesus.* We met for several months together. Most of those women, plus others they brought, found new life in Christ. Others were greatly strengthened in their faith by their ministry to one another.

Only two have come with their families to Our Heritage Church. Most have not. But Christ is real to them where He was not before. Many are more involved in the life of their own churches than they ever were before.

The group dissolved sometime ago. But now Gloria and another friend from that group (neither of them are involved in evangelical churches) have begun a new little church among

[17] Some informative suggestions that we found very helpful in starting and conducting evangelistic home Bible study groups are contained in a paper produced by the Lay Division of Campus Crusade for Christ. See Appendix I.

[18] Glen Eyrie, Colorado Springs, Colorado.

[19] Box 11, South Holland, Illinois 60473.

their "non-evangelical" friends. There is a continuing "live" witness for the living Jesus in a place where no evangelical pastor's ministry could reach.

That's one story of many.

Other Beginnings

About thirty little churches now meet regularly around our neighborhood. More people are involved in these groups than in Sunday school or morning worship. Most involve people who are not members or attenders of Our Heritage, as well as those who are a part of the church.

Most groups meet in homes. But some meet in restaurants, or on school campuses.

Many were started through pastoral encouragement, assistance and organization. In some, either Carl or I led the group until it was ready to assume its own leadership.

But a growing number of these little churches are beginning spontaneously, as the Holy Spirit lays upon the heart of some Christian the spiritual needs of his/her/their neighbors. In the past six months, five groups have started that way. I was not told until after they had started, or after the plans were well underway. All five began as "evangelistic groups." Most will evolve into permanent little churches.

In some groups, we have used the famous *Quaker Questions* as a "self-starter" to group sharing. These questions probe immediately *below the surface* to the real people involved. Before we begin to study the Bible together, we take most of the first meeting to let each person answer these questions:

1. Where did you live between the ages of seven and twelve?
2. How many brothers and sisters did you have?
3. How did your family heat your house at that time?
4. Where was the center of *human warmth* in your home?
5. When, in your life, did God become more than just a word to you? [20]

[20] For a more detailed description of how to use these questions to start a group see *Groups That Work*, a compilation published by Zondervan. See Chapter 2, pp. 16-19, by Keith Miller.

We allow every member of the group to answer the first question before going on to the second, etc.

This series of simple questions gets the group acquainted and sharing on a very *personal level,* immediately. It's a good introduction to a group experience that deals with persons and their needs, instead of being little more than an exchange of surface opinions and ideas about the Bible.

Who Leads?

Some groups are "leaderless." The entire group is committed (unofficially) to the purpose of getting to know Christ better. As they look into the Word, they depend on the Spirit to lead the group. In a leaderless group, the host usually opens the meeting and closes it. But the *group* leads, teaches, counsels, and "polices" itself, making all its own decisions on a consensus basis. The Spirit is given maximum freedom to be "Head" of a "leaderless" group.

A few groups have a leader who especially prepares and does a minimum of "teaching," by supplying background material and leading discussion. But even in these groups, the emphasis is on involvement and freedom. The group still ministers. Each member exercises his gift for the benefit of all.

There is a place for formal teaching and preaching in the church, but only rarely is that place in these groups. Group meetings are for the priesthood to function. They are for soul-fellowship, for problem-solving, mutual care, and sharing life in Christ together.

Several groups were led for a time by the pastor whose purpose is always to "work himself out of a job" as quickly as possible. The leadership of the Spirit and the responsiveness and development of the group, not any arbitrary rule, determine when pastoral leadership ends.

Leaders receive their training informally by personal participation in group life, usually without knowing they are being trained. The Spirit chooses those He will to whom to impart leadership gifts. In time, the group's "chosen" leader emerges. We simply have to be sensitive enough to the Spirit to recognize his gifts.

Recently, when one of the little churches met, it was discovered that the designated leader for the evening was out of town. His wife was asked by someone if she would lead. She declined and pushed an open Bible into the hands of the new Christian sitting next to her.

"Well, what do I do?" he asked.

"Start reading," someone suggested.

So he began to read. After just two verses, he stopped and said thoughtfully: "My life isn't like that – not at all! How easy it is to read it, but how hard it is to put it into practice!"

The group was off! This is exactly what it takes to make a group really click on a personal level. From that moment on, the only leader needed was the Spirit.

Authority

Once they get started, the groups are somewhat autonomous. Church board and pastor exercise authority over them, but it is not an "official" authority. It is only a "spiritual" authority. Yet, while they do not have to recognize it at all if they don't want to, for the most part the little churches are responsive to any rebuke, reproof, instruction and correction that is given. In turn, they feel free to offer loving correction and rebuke to "mother church" and pastor.

We do not have a "group coordinator" to oversee group life.

Curriculum

The "curriculum" is another thing left to the discretion of the group itself.

Many of our groups started on Campus Crusade's *Ten Basic Steps to Christian Maturity*. None have ever completed the *Steps*. After one or two of these booklets (no group ever studied more than four), the group became anxious to get more *directly* into the Bible itself.

What they study and how they are to study it is decided by the group. Infrequently, they will use material prepared for Sunday school use. One group went through Keith Miller's *A Taste of New Wine* together. Two women's groups centered their study around Hannah Whitehall Smith's *The Christian's Secret of a Happy Life.* But most bring their lives to weekly paragraph-by-paragraph discussion of the *raw Word* — the Bible speaking for itself.

If the group decides to do it, they may ask the host for each week (most of the groups move from house to house) to choose the passage for study. Most of the little churches, however, choose a book (one of the gospels, Acts, one of the epistles, etc.) and proceed through it at the rate of about one chapter a week (though if the group hangs up on one verse and spends the whole session there, it is no disaster).

Sometimes, as our groups work through a passage, there will be as many as eight different translations or paraphrases around the circle. Pulling these together helps to give the group the whole sense of the passage's meaning.

Though there is always a certain amount of discussion of impersonal facts and ideas, the discussions bring the teachings of the Word into focus in *life* as the members of the group are living it day after day. Personal experiences, problems and feelings are shared in the light of God's Word. Open expression of doubts, fears, failures to "measure up," serious questions about the meaning or practicability of the passage, are a part of *ministering* to one another in the group. Participants come to know each other rather well. The person behind the facade comes into view. When this happens, the Holy Spirit can guide human hearts in caring redemptively for one another.

Conversational prayer often deals with things shared during the Bible study.

How Big Is a Little Church?

Jesus said, "If *two* of you shall agree on earth as touching anything that they shall ask, it shall be done for them of my Father which is in heaven. For where *two or three are gathered together in my name,* there am I in the midst of them" (Matthew 18:19-20, italics mine).

Two or three Christians is enough to experience some degree of Body life.

When a group reaches more than twelve, some will stop talking and just listen. They will not share, they will only *receive*. (It's like Sunday morning church again!) As the size of the group reaches fourteen or more, some will begin to feel that the group is not meeting their needs or doesn't really need their contribution any more, so they will become irregular in attendance and then simply drop out altogether.

The most effective group size is seven to twelve people. We will start a little church with as few as three.

When a group grows to thirteen active members, it should pray about starting a second group. A new little church can be formed by simply dividing the present group in two. This can sometimes be done on the basis of geography, if the group is willing.

One of the best suggestions is for the little church to look upon the new group to be formed from them as an "outreach," not as a "division." After discussing the need for a second group and reasons for it, they should pray that the Holy Spirit would place it on the hearts of some members of the group to volunteer to be the nucleus of a new little church. The "old" group would "mother" the new one, through prayer, encouragement and moral support.

Where The Groups Have Failed

The little churches, as a whole, have resulted in new life for the church and its constituents.[21]

However, there have been failures. And any church that decides to move in this direction should expect failures. Just as individual believers often stop short of total surrender to the Lordship of Christ, small groups also miss the mark and die.

Early in our "small group ministry," if a group I had worked to start did not make it, I would be crushed. But as experience has grown and the Spirit has enlightened me, I have found myself saying, "Thank You, Lord," as I've watched one group and then another have its last meeting, fizzle out and quietly disappear from the life of the church.

For it is always an *unhealthy* little church that dies.

[21] See Chapter 11

Whenever a group finds its oneness in the flesh (they meet together not for the primary purpose of knowing Christ better, but because they are friends) you can count on it – that group will sooner or later expire. The flesh can maintain it for a while, but ultimately, the group built around the flesh will dissolve.

If sharing degenerates to gossiping, the group will destroy itself.

I have seen spiritual pride ravage a group until it fell apart.

Groups formed out of divisive motives, from their outset have a divisive spirit. Unless genuine repentance has come, in which this spirit has changed, such groups have lasted for a while, but then they have become pointless, impotent. And they have passed from the scene.

I have been involved in little churches that seemed really to be flourishing. People seemed to be coming alive spiritually. Jesus was becoming real to the members. But as the light of the Word increased and the Spirit called for surrender to Jesus as unquestioned *Lord of all of life,* the group stopped short of that level of surrender, struggled for its life for a while, and then fell apart through neglect.

Another group kept going for more than two years, in spite of the fact that they never learned really to share Life together. It was a Bible study – little more. It rejected its role as "the Body," as priests to one another. Its members refused to get "that involved" with one another. Its discussions were mainly on an "idea level" rather than a personal level. I was amazed that it could keep going for so long with no more visible life than it had. But eventually, it dwindled to the two or three who were responsive to the Spirit, and then, graciously, the Spirit built a whole new group on the old foundation. But the old, impersonal group had to die.

When a group dies, its members who still want a group experience usually find their way into another group.

These failures and deaths are not tragedies at all. They are like a natural abortion, in which the mother's body mercifully expels a malformed or unhealthy fetus. This may seem like a tragedy at the time. But actually it is the family's salvation from a life-long heartache.

It is part of the way the Spirit can be trusted to build His living church.

Of course, there are also imperfections in the living groups that we would like to see perfected.

Sometimes they fail to become very deeply personal, to catch a spirit of openness with one another, where deep needs can be honestly exposed, and deep, fervent *agapé*-love can flourish.

Sometimes a group will fail to see itself as "the church." It is still too dependent on the institution who mothered it and the pastor and agencies of that institution. Consequently, the believer-priesthood doesn't function as effectively as it could, if they saw themselves as really responsible and capable of needed spiritual ministry to one another. Sometimes they wait for leadership from the mother church or pastor when they should go ahead, under the leadership of the Holy Spirit, into evangelism and service to others outside their group.

Occasionally the members of a group will cling too tightly to the bond of fellowship they enjoy, which is very precious to them after a while. They will fail to divide or, in some other way, to start a new group when the time to do so was strategic. It is a traumatic experience, but done in the Spirit, it can enhance both spiritual maturity within the group and growth of the Body.

An additional failure has been our inability to get all Christians in our church constituency involved in group life. There are a number who, though outwardly sympathetic to renewal, the building of little churches, and the results to our congregation, have never chosen to get personally involved in this type of fellowship.

I have tried to answer here most of the questions that are asked me concerning small groups in the church. Others will be answered in the course of the following chapters.

There are observers of the current scene who are fearful that the time is not far distant when the church in the Western World may have to live under a totalitarian government either from the far left or the far right. History abounds with warnings that the church under such a regime may face the necessity of having to function as the church, *without* buildings, pastors, conventional organizational structure, or any of the things most feel are so necessary to church life today. When that day comes, the church which has taught its people to minister to each other and to function as the living Body of Christ, in utter dependence upon the Holy Spirit for its life and leadership, will be *the last to die.*

But it is more than future protection that causes me to be excited about the ministry of believers sharing fellowship from house to house. There is something very existential. Something is happening *now.*

While it is still so imperfect, so embryonic, so incomplete compared with that full-blown picture of it in the New Testament, this infant church is experiencing a genuine foretaste of that *same spontaneous, Spirit-born LIFE.*

XI

TOUCHING THE FRINGES OF LIFE

I WOULD be foolish to claim that Our Heritage is a "New Testament Church." It is still too "institutional," too "organizational," too clearly the "established church."

But it *can truthfully* be called "the church *in transition*."

Renewal is "in process." Change is evident. The new life is nearly tangible. The mark of the Holy Spirit can be seen on the fellowship.

Things are different now from what they were three or four years ago. Decidedly different. Blessedly different. Excitingly different.

Our "renewal story" has only begun to be written . . . but it *has begun.*

We do not yet have full blown New Testament-style church life . . . but we are *touching the fringes of that Life.*

To an ever-increasing number of people in our town, Jesus Christ is living reality. They can tell you how He's working in their lives *today*. They see His hand in everything that happens to them. They wake up each morning anticipating the new things He will do in their lives that day.

They can tell you how they have seen Him alive and at work in the lives of others. They can tell of answers to prayer, of evidences of Christ's presence, of some new thing He's been teaching them.

They can tell you how God is using the very difficult problem they are facing to do something in their lives.

And they can tell you they are not alone.

The "small group ministry" sparked from Our Heritage now encompasses an estimated three hundred people (mostly adults), meeting in more than forty homes each week to study the Word, share the experiences of life in Christ together, and to pray.

More than half of these are still connected with Our Heritage. Many are part of the new Circle Wesleyan Church,[1] a "pioneer" congregation using renewal principles, begun from Our Heritage. A few are groups to which we gave birth, but which are no longer connected with our fellowship, which in no way takes away from the ministry of Life they share.

These group fellowships never end. Throughout the week the members minister to one another through prayer and helpful service.

On Sunday morning most of the group members gather (at the chapel, in our case) to share in the larger Body-fellowship and to receive the teaching of the Word.

Opportunity is given there for sharing of the things that are happening as they take Christ through the nitty-gritty of everyday life.

They hear sermons designed to teach the doctrines of the Bible, and to show them how to live life in the Spirit, as individuals, as groups and as a congregation.

They seldom hear an evangelistic sermon. For the benefit of the uncommitted who are present, however, there often is an explanation of what it means to receive Jesus Christ as Savior.

Celebration of the Lord's Supper is informal and personal and anticipated with joy. Baptism, mostly by immersion, (though not always), is a part of the Sunday morning meeting and is an edifying experience for the whole congregation.

Though public "come-forward" invitations are rare, there is a *constant flow of new converts,* giving testimony in the groups and in the congregation, presenting themselves for baptism or for church membership, or being reported by those the Spirit used to lead them to Christ.

[1] The story of Circle Church is in Chapter 14.

And whenever the Body gathers — in groups or in the congregation — the key thrust is fellowship — soul-fellowship.

If the meetings have a musical theme, it is the Catholic folk song we sing every Sunday morning and often at other times:

> We are one in the Spirit, We are one in the Lord,
> We are one in the Spirit, We are one in the Lord,
> And we pray that all unity may one day be restored;
> And they'll know we are Christians by our love, by our love,
> Yes, they'll know we are Christians by our love.
>
> We will walk with each other, we will walk hand in hand,
> We will walk with each other, we will walk hand in hand,
> And together we'll spread the news that God is in our land;
> And they'll know we are Christians by our love, by our love.
> Yes, they'll know we are Christians by our love.
>
> All praise to the Father from whom all things come,
> And all praise to Christ Jesus, His only Son,
> And all praise to the Spirit who makes us one;
> And they'll know we are Christians by our love, by our love,
> Yes, they'll know we are Christians by our love. *

They Talk About Jesus

While not everyone in the church constituency is a Christian yet, in the sense of having committed their lives to Christ, and while not all are involved in group life, if one engages another in conversation, chances are they will not have talked long before they are talking about what the Lord is doing.

Jesus is real to these people. He is alive. He acts and they see it. He speaks and they hear it. He leads. He disciplines. He teaches. He loves. He is working in their lives. He is working in their group and in their church.

Sharing in the groups sets tongues loose to talk about the Lord.

They sit together in homes and in natural speech, everyday terms, converse about the Lord Jesus. There is no stained glass or organ strains there to confuse the issue. There is just the raw Word, my life as it really is, and a group of friends who know me better than most people do.

* Written by Peter Scholtes. Copyright © 1966 by F. E. L. Publications, Ltd., 1543 W. Olympic Blvd., Los Angeles, Cal. 90015. Used by permission.

And we talk about Jesus. About who He is. About what He did. Mostly about what He is doing now in our lives.

If I haven't decided before I get into the group, soon I am confronted with the decision. Is Jesus alive and real, or isn't He? Is what the Bible says about Him true, or isn't it?

In a group of people who are talking about Him as if He was right there, I can't go on long without making that decision.

Once I decide that He is alive and real, I talk about Him, too. (In fact, in the group I will talk about Him even before that decision.) It soon becomes as natural to talk about Jesus as about my family. And to talk about Him in *natural*, everyday, conversational terms.

Soon we begin talking about Him with the family at home – naturally.

Whenever we get together with other believers we talk about Him. No one has to say, "The church meeting will now begin." It doesn't have to be a "church meeting." Whenever two Christians get together they talk about Jesus.

They Care About Each Other

They know about each other. They know each other better than the people of any church with which I have ever had anything to do. And because of this knowledge and their personal knowledge and acceptance of the love of Christ, they are learning, falteringly, little by little to love one another with a deep kind of love.

Their group meetings never end. If a problem is mentioned in the meeting, chances are someone will call during the week and say, "I'm praying for you."

If someone misses a meeting, they either will have already called and told why, or someone will check with them to see if they are all right. Absent members are prayed for by name and problem.

The telephone lines keep the fellowship going through the week. Advice on every level from how to grow African daisies, to living with teenagers, to husband-wife relationships are shared.

A typical phone call between group members begins, "Hey! I

was reading my Bible this morning, and God gave me a beautiful promise for you and the problem you're facing. . . ."

Much pastoral counseling is cared for by the groups themselves. Most of my present counseling load consists of people with the most serious of problems or with people not involved in group life.

Though it lacks perfection, there is an attitude of acceptance in the fellowship.

In the groups (especially the new ones), a person can *say anything* – even if his opinion may not be scriptural.

Recently Carl told me about a new group he was leading. In the first meeting, two sharp new men took exception to his references to a *personal devil*. They declared that they didn't believe in the devil. Carl didn't argue, he simply said, "All right, let me refer then to an 'evil influence' in the world . . .," and then went on with his point.

The men stayed with the group, came alive in Christ, and a few weeks later were talking about the problems they were having with the (*personal*) *devil!*

A person may be anything and find acceptance in the groups and in the congregation.

Kids on drugs sometimes come to the teenage "Bible rap." Length of hair makes no difference whatsoever. Both "short hairs" and "long hairs" hold important leadership positions in the church. Barefoot youth, girls in slacks and shorts, boys in "grubby" jeans, find acceptance in the church services.

New Christians are heard, occasionally, using "profanity" to emphasize a point in a Bible study. I have never seen anything but acceptance and willingness to simply overlook such a lapse.

Blacks and whites fellowship deeply with one another. Scottsdale is a nearly "lily-white" suburb, with only a few black families. Some of these families have become a part of our church family. Their fellowship and ministry in the Body are highly valued, especially in the instances where they have joined in the life of the groups.

Love between Christians is real and growing. It is freely expressed. It is not uncommon to see two people hugging each other in a spontaneous expression of brotherly love reminiscent of Paul's instructions for the Corinthians to "greet one another with a holy kiss."[1]

Never in all my years as a minister of the Gospel have I been told so often, "Pastor, I love you." Seldom does a week go by without my hearing such an expression.

One of the most important direct benefits of this caring, acceptance and expression of love between brothers and sisters in Jesus, is that they more quickly come to know and accept the fact that *God loves them.*

They Pray

Earlier, I stated that my wife and I felt alone in prayer.[2] It seemed at that time that, while I preached on prayer and asked people to pray – *no one prayed.*

I don't preach nearly so much on prayer today – yet more people are praying. And their prayers are being answered.

About two hundred people per week join together in Our Heritage-sponsored meetings that are designed so that a very important place is given to conversational prayer. That's more people than are in church Sunday morning.

More people in prayer meetings than attending Sunday school or morning worship! I never thought I'd see the day.

They Share Their Faith

A member of one of the little churches was telling a group of ministers about her group. Someone asked her about witnessing. She explained how it works.

"In our meetings we talk about Jesus," she said. "You have to decide for yourself if Christ is real. Does the Bible really mean what it says? Is Jesus Christ alive or isn't He? If He is alive, what does that mean in *my* life? As we study and as we share from week to week, we see that He is doing things in our lives that we had never seen before. A neighbor comes over and shares

[1] 1 Corinthians 16:20
[2] Chapter 1, p. 18

a problem with us. Pretty soon, in helping with the problem, we are talking about Jesus.

"And *before we know it, we have witnessed!*"

Acts 1:8 is a promise, not a demand. "You shall receive power after that the Holy Ghost is come upon you, and you *shall be witnesses unto me.*"

The key to witnessing has never been to train the flesh how to witness. The key since century one has *always* been, to get the Christian so full of Jesus, so full of the Holy Spirit, that those around him are caught in the spontaneous overflow.

Filling with the Spirit is not a once-and-for-all thing. That is why Paul used the passive voice in Ephesians 5:18, where a literal translation from the Greek would have to read, "Be ye *being filled* with the Holy Spirit."

Life in small groups (or some other structure which allows the members of the Body to function in mutual ministry) helps to keep the believer open and surrendered for the continual filling of the Spirit.

Kept full, he witnesses. It becomes a spontaneous work of the Spirit in and through him.

They See Miracles

Here are just a few: a housewife cured of stomach ulcers in answer to united prayer. A woman who entered the hospital for kidney surgery, but when the time came to operate, only scars on her kidney hinted that there had ever been a problem. The pastor miraculously healed of prostitus just days before surgery, in answer to simple prayer. A malignancy behind a small boy's eye, bulging it visibly, after group prayer turned out to be a harmless cyst. An alcoholic husband and father delivered from the disease upon receiving Christ. [3]

The answer to one person's deep problem came miraculously in a meaningful dream, in which clear instructions were given. [4]

Demons have been cast out. [5]

[3] James 5:15
[4] Acts 2:17
[5] Mark 16:17

There was a young microbiologist who had received no help from seven psychiatrists. She was driven uncontrollably by a second evil personality using her body. She was set free within two weeks from the time we commanded, in the name of Jesus, that the demon leave her body. Then, she saw a Christian psychiatrist and received great help.

Audrey and I, who prayed with her, had never been involved in anything like this before. But Christ has become so real these past years that we are now open to whatever the Bible teaches about such things.

In another instance, a "hopeless" alcoholic received the will to quit and to be rehabilitated after demons were commanded to leave.

One woman, with a fifteen-year drug-abuse problem, was changed and delivered through the prayers of a group of ladies.

Through "two or three gathered together in my name," agreeing in prayer, financial needs have been supplied, homes have been saved from divorce, teenagers and their parents have been reconciled, men and women and young people have come to know Jesus Christ, and trouble has turned out to be a tremendous blessing.

They Engage in Service

While mutual helpfulness among members of the groups is evident, selfless service outside the group is still in its early growing stages. But what the people do carry out, in the church as an organization, in interchurch service, and in Christian social involvement is *not phony or forced,* it is *real.* It flows from genuine Spirit-ignited love and concern – not from pressure or "law."

As pastor, I will wait for the Spirit to ignite the fires of such service, rather than resort to "putting the bite on." Because when helpful service flows from a heart saying "Yes" to the Spirit, it's valuable, powerful, effective service. It's beautiful. Not always "refined," but beautiful.

They Grow

Involved in group life, and seeing Christ as very personal and certainly alive, people grow. And their growth can be seen.

Their growth in Christ is in no way stunted by the limitations of a one-man, one-gift ministry, as it was before renewal began, before the "little churches" were born.

Each believer has gifts to be used in ministry to the other members and to the Body. The groups give opportunity for discovery and use of these gifts. (And *all* the gifts listen in 1 Corinthians 12, Ephesians 4 and Romans 12 are evident somewhere in our fellowship.)

As more and more people have opportunity to minister with their gift or gifts, Christ becomes more real, knowledge of the Truth is expanded, faith is increased, sensitivity to the Spirit is sharpened, submission to the will of God is deepened, and spiritual spontaneity in life as a Christian is spotlighted.

People learn to walk one-to-one with the Spirit of Jesus. They no longer wait for the pastor or the organized church to give them somehing to do. They find their own ministry of life under the leadership of the Holy Spirit. Sometimes this involves them in the organizational framework of the church. Often it does not.

As long as I kept them tied to me or to the institution, they could only grow within that narrow framework. Once set free to the ministry of the Spirit and the Body — the extent of their spiritual growth is limited only by their own responsiveness to the will of God. They can grow past me. They can grow past the institution. "Growing up into Christ in all things." [6]

The groups have been the key to such growth.

"I didn't realize what the Bible study (group) had done in my life," said a housewife-beautician in her twenties, "until a year after I joined the group, and the people at work told me they could see the difference."

They Trust the Lord

Instead of fighting the circumstances and problems of life, the groups have helped to create a view of life which sees how God is able to use *everything* and *anything* that happens in the life of a Christian to accomplish good and precious changes that could not have come any other way.

[6] Ephesians 4:15

The key Bible passage on which this view is based is Romans 8:28.

> We are assured and know that (God being a partner in their labor) *all things* work together and are (fitting into a plan) for good to those who love God and are called according to (His) design and purpose (Romans 8:28, Amplified New Testament. Italics mine).

The groups aid in this view by being a sharing-place for the problems, reverses and pressures of daily living. Together, they watch and pray for one another as they go through these things. And soon, through its sharing and bearing together, the group is able to *see* some of the "good" that comes to the Christian life from the difficulties encountered. As they see this promise proven true again and again, they are practically driven to the conviction that it is dependable.

Until . . .

A young woman was kidnaped and raped last year. But she kept rejoicing in the way God was using the "tragedy of it" to make her unconverted family listen to her testimony about Jesus.

A man's father died. While personally sorrowing, the man could "hardly wait" to see how God was going to be able to use this in the lives of his relatives who did not know the Lord.

Parents, whose teenager was arrested on a charge of "possession and use of dangerous drugs," while greatly disappointed and shocked, were thanking God for it, because they knew it was going to open a closed door in their relationship with the child.

Even when the "good" is not so clearly visible, there has developed a spirit of anticipation and thankfulness and trust that operates in every possible situation, problem, pain or pressure. There is a sense of expectancy and sure knowledge that *when trouble comes God is working.*

If the one who is directly involved in the trouble has difficulty claiming Romans 8:28, the group claims it for him. And they support and encourage him until he can trust for himself.

These people, immature and weak in faith though they may yet be, together see "all things" as flowing from the loving hand of an all-wise Father, who knows just what the deepest need of His child is, and acts to meet that need.

They Have LIFE!

For the most part, these "group people" see Jesus as alive and His Spirit as living in them.

They are conscious of that Life. It is evident to them when they sin and are made deeply aware of it. It is evident to them as they share that life with their brothers and sisters in Jesus — and can see Him at work in each other's lives.

They are also conscious of the life of the Body. Some experience this "Body-consciousness" more than others.

There are those with the gift of discernment who can sense any rift, any ripple of individualism or discord within the group. Even though they may not be directly involved, they are pained deeply until the oneness is restored again, through confession, forgiveness or obedience. During the duration of the problem, they often agonize in prayer until the unity is restored.

This is discernment. Watchman Nee calls it "Body-consciousness." It is a sign of Life.

There's a spontaneity of life that is definitely New Testament in character. Things happen that I do not push or plan. The Spirit has freedom to direct *His* program. He sends this one here. He hinders that one from going. He puts into this person's life those people who can edify him the most.

A Jehovah's Witness creates confusion in a new Christian's mind. The Spirit sends a former Jehovah's Witness, converted to Christ, to help her.

Here's someone who needs a bit of loving reproof. I can see it, but I wait for the Spirit. He sends just the right one to do the job.

Here is a neighborhood that is ripe for the ministry of a small evangelistic group. The Spirit, without my help, lays the burden for the neighbors on the heart of some Christian living there. Soon a group has been started. People are being won to Christ. The Spirit did it.

This group seems to be getting out into "left field" doctrinally.

My first impulse is to invade the group and wipe out the heresy single-handedly. But I wait and pray that the Spirit, who has some responsive people in that group, will do it His way through them. In His time, He does it. And it is beautiful.

I need to talk with a brother about a problem, but I don't know when is the right time to go to him, and besides I don't have time. So the Spirit sends him to me. One time might be labeled a coincidence. But this happens time after time.

I need help on some very "institutional" project. I don't know to whom to go. So, the Spirit leads just the right person to call and volunteer.

More and more the people of Our Heritage, and their pastor, can see the Spirit building and shaping the church and its fellowship in His own inimitable way.

There's Life there.

It's not the full garment of His Life filling all and controlling all. It's only the *fringe*. There is so much more of it to have. He wants His Life to be all we count on, all we look for, all we want. That's not the case yet.

But, thank God, He has lovingly, patiently re-formed us until He could put us in touch with, at least

. . . *The fringes of Life.*

XII

POTPOURRI

EVANGELISM

THE USUAL approach to getting Christians to share their faith is to (1) train them in the use of some evangelistic procedure (such as *The Four Spiritual Laws*), and then (2) *keep the pressure on* so they'll feel "properly condemned" if they don't use the training they've been given.

Before we ever began to think about renewal, we already felt that training alone was not enough to make mature witnesses and evangelists out of rank-and-file Christians. We had seen a number of our members come back all steamed up from Lay Institute Training in personal evangelism, only to have that head of steam cool to a powerless dribble in an amazingly short period of time.

We have found that the believer who sees Jesus as alive in him and as active in his life to meet his real needs will witness . . . almost automatically.

I think it can be quite easily shown from Scripture that every Christian will be a witness, if the Holy Spirit is in his life (Acts 1:8). Romans 8:9 indicates that the Holy Spirit *is* in the life of everyone who belongs to Jesus Christ. It is logical to believe that the more control the Spirit is given in a Christian's life, the more useful that life will be as a witness to Jesus Christ.

But while everyone upon whom the Holy Spirit dwells will surely be a witness, *not every Christian is gifted by the Spirit as an "evangelist."* According to Ephesians 4:11, "some" are. Just as "some" are "apostles," "some" are prophets, and "some" are "pastors and teachers."

All are witnesses. The church needs the witness of all if it is to reach its world. But to force all to be evangelists, is to make something happen that Christ Himself has not planned.

I'm afraid this is what we have been trying to do, especially in these recent years, when the *very needed* emphasis on personal evangelism has been hitting its peak.

I just came away from a meeting with a dear friend who is part of a great evangelistic organization which concentrates on college campuses. It's not difficult for me to feel guilt. And to succumb to pressures, especially in the direction of programs for evangelism, underscored by numerous references to the Great Commission. It seems each organization has its well-meaning, "Spirit-directed" *boxes* into which every Christian must fit.

We cannot say we have confronted *every* person in our immediate area with an opportunity to know Christ. Even though the people who live fence-to-fence with many of our Christians *do* know that the difference in their lives is Christ. And when trouble strikes in many of the blocks in our area, our Christian in the block is the one they come to for help and understanding. We have also placed evangelistic literature in most homes in our immediate area.

But . . . every door has not been knocked on. *The Four Spiritual Laws* has not been presented to every person. Even in my own block this is true.

Yes . . . more, *much more* needs to be done. The Great Commission *does* have to be fulfilled. "God is not willing that *any* should perish, but that *all* should come to repentance." [1]

But does that mean . . . that this task, the task of evangelism, is exempt from "the law of the Spirit of life in Christ Jesus"? [2] And because it is not being done in the Spirit (at least it looks that way to some) should we now move into the challenge with the human leverage of *legalism* to get the job done?

[1] 2 Peter 3:9 (italics mine)
[2] Romans 8:2

If life in the Spirit fails to produce witnesses and evangelists—can we (*should* we) produce them by the coercion of law? Doesn't Acts 1:8 say that even the fulfilling of the Great Commission is not to be a thing of human effort but a spontaneous act of the Spirit in and through Spirit-filled people?

I needed to write this just to get a fresh grip on the truth. For I am an easy target for those who are full of genuine zeal for soul-winning, who, in all honesty, before the Lord, are convinced that to do it in the flesh is better than not to do it at all. (They can present a pretty convincing case for this.) Cannot the Spirit be trusted to thrust laborers into the harvest, just as surely as He can be trusted to prepare the hearts to whom they go?

It may seem slower and less existential to take the time to build disciples who are free to follow the Spirit and to be placed by Him where and when His program calls for it. But somehow, I believe that even if it takes longer to go that route, it is of greater eternal value to have *the Spirit doing the work* through the few who will let Him do it, than to have many trying to do the Spirit's work *in the energy of the flesh,* and then claiming God's work has been done, when in reality it has been mostly *man's work.*

The New Testament describes three basic kinds of evangelism.

Mass evangelism. One man speaking to the crowd. Jesus and the five thousand. Peter at Pentecost, "drawing the net," and baptizing 3,000 in a single day. Philip at Samaria. Peter, again, in the house of Cornelius. Paul on Mars Hill. Until recent years this was thought by many Christians to be almost the *only* way to win men. Get them to come to a "revival" meeting. Give invitations at Sunday morning or Sunday evening services. But it has been many years since the unconverted could be attracted in significant numbers to any of these. Still, there *is* a place for mass evangelism today.

There needs to be a rethinking of our methods. Many things we require people to do "in public" constitute *additions to the requirements of the Gospel.*

For instance, we evangelicals make it necessary for a person who is seeking to know Christ to "come forward" to an altar or prayer room. Thus, before he scarcely believes, he has to cross an *artificial barrier* to come to Christ. If he is an extrovert and is not afraid of the "unknown" (i.e., the interior of the prayer room or what goes on at the altar), he has a better chance of being saved. If he is an introvert or has any doubts, it may be years before he finds enough courage to "take that first step."

Altar calls are rare at Our Heritage. I have given no more than six or eight invitations to "come forward" in my six years as pastor.

At the beginning, I intended to make a practice of it. I wanted so badly to be able to report so many "decisions" each Sunday – like my successful colleagues did. But every time I gave an invitation the free spirit in our fellowship seemed to be squelched. A coldness and hardness moved in to spoil the warmth and openness we shared together. I could almost "see" the artificial barrier I was erecting. The Spirit was saying, "No."

We felt this so strongly (though no one contradicted the practice) that I knew that, at Our Heritage, I would be sinning if I persisted.

Since this discovery, I have given invitations *only* at events where the make-up of the crowd seemed to warrant it: a church-sponsored "concert under the stars" at a public park; back-to-back Sunday afternoon and evening showings at the church of a recent Billy Graham film. Even in such cases as these I feel it will be better when we have sufficient volunteers to be able to give a non-public invitation, in which interested persons sign cards and are followed up personally in their homes.

In our Sunday morning meetings we encourage unbelievers present to invite Christ into their lives and then to let someone else know about it. "I'm always available to answer your questions about knowing Christ in a personal way."

They do it. One by one. They make private decisions to receive Christ and then declare it publicly, telling their family, their group, or me, or presenting themselves for baptism or church membership, or sharing testimony in a public gathering.

We trust the Spirit to be faithful to them and to draw them to

Jesus. And He does it – without the barrier of a public invitation.

Of course, there is one problem with this approach. When people come to Christ solely through the faithfulness of the Spirit, no one else can take the credit!

Personal evangelism. Man to man. Conversational evangelism. Jesus with the Samaritan divorcee. Philip hitch-hiking with the treasurer of the Ethiopian government. A time and place for give-and-take, question-and-answer, eyeball-to-eyeball.

Christ has given our fellowship some personal evangelists, and He is constantly adding to the church through them. I thank God for the immense help in this area given by Campus Crusade for Christ. I have, personally, had the privilege of seeing scores of people who came to me for counsel find Christ through the simple explanation found in *The Four Spiritual Laws.*

Body evangelism. Not much is said about this kind of evangelism, but it is predominant in the "book of Acts."[3]

Peter Gillquist in his book, *Love Is Now,* describes "Body evangelism" as the kind of evangelism

> . . . where the body of Christ is moving under the direction of the Holy Spirit and new life inevitably results. It is the "and the Lord was adding to their number day by day those who were being saved" type of outreach.[4]
> God was so real in their midst, that becoming a part of their fellowship was tantamount to receiving Jesus Christ, and receiving Jesus Christ meant, by the same token, a new identity with God's people.[5]

As many people have come to Christ through simply associating with the church and its groups as by personal evangelism.

They start as interested pagans attending one of the little churches, and before long they are talking about what Christ is doing in their lives. No one pressured them or "prayed with" them, or even particularly "shared" with them. But they received

[3] Acts 2:47
[4] Peter Gillquist, *Love Is Now* (Grand Rapids: Zondervan Publishing House), p. 115.
[5] Ibid., p. 116.

the fellowship and were received by the fellowship and seemed simply to "catch" faith. A few cannot even tell about the moment they received Christ. They just know He is alive in them. The fruits are there, so who can deny it?

Quietly, by ones and twos, the Lord has been adding to His Church. In the past two years, our segment of the Body of Christ has reproduced itself. More have been led to Christ than were in the church two years ago.

Many have joined as members of the church. Many have not. Many were told, "Go back to your own people and your own church and witness there." Many are in the little churches but not yet in the congregation. Some find fellowship and growth in a little church and worship on Sunday with their families at Catholic, Lutheran, Congregational, Methodist and other churches.

The Body is being built. We welcome those the Lord gives us.

If we have a "strategy" for evangelizing our town it is this:

1. The proliferation of small groups throughout the city as the Lord gives us people in each neighborhood.
2. The establishment of new congregations, using a nucleus of Spirit-chosen people from the "mother church." Each new congregation develops small groups and eventually reaches out to establish new congregations from itself.
3. Emphasis on personal witnessing and evangelism as the Spirit leads. Training is offered, but not forced upon anyone.
4. As the Lord supplies people and funds (or faith), to use all media and all means at our disposal to get the Good News about Jesus into every home in our area. (Literature, radio, television, newspapers – even door-to-door witnessing, if the Spirit gives us those with this gift.)

Jesus said of His kingdom, it is like "leaven, which a woman took and hid in three measures of meal, till the whole was leavened."[6] This is, in part, a picture of the evangelistic strategy

[6] Matthew 13:33

of the Holy Spirit. Through God's people, under the leadership of the Spirit, the Gospel spreads from person to person until the kingdom permeates the entire community.

Missions

If a church is in good spiritual health, according to First Corinthians 16 and Second Corinthians 8 and 9, its heart and purse are easily opened to meet the needs of brothers and sisters in Christ in hard pressed and underdeveloped areas of the world.

As we planned and prayed for the new church, we prayed that that kind of "missionary spirit" would be part of it.

The church was nearly *six years old!* Far past the age when a church ought to start reaching out to meet the needs of others outside itself.

Several missionaries had visited us. Their services were poorly attended and just didn't "click." Nothing significant happened.

We had laid tentative plans for a week-long "missions conference" a couple of times, but they failed to materialize.

We'll plan one soon, I told myself.

But God did it all by Himself, with a minimum of sweat and strain on my part. He moved swiftly and when it was over, the whole church was amazed at what *He* had done and *how* He had done it.

Our denominational World Missions Department dispatched a couple of missionaries to do deputation work in our district. Each church would be visited. One missionary would hold one service in each church. An offering would be taken.

It all sounded so familiar. We'd done it all before. So we made no unusual plans. I saw it as fulfilling a denominational obligation. But I was frankly skeptical as to the spiritual possibilities of such a service.

Not knowing the man who was to come, I hoped he would not be a "legalist" or long-winded. I was anything but optimistic. But I felt we needed exposure to our denomination's foreign mission program.

When the missionary to Zambia arrived, the Spirit began to do some amazing things — in His divine ways which are so astounding that Paul declared them to be "past finding out."[7]

He was a likable young man, at first, with an intriguing Newfoundland accent. But he dropped a bomb in my lap and aroused all my old fears of legalism and life under the law when he announced that, in spite of the fact that I had publicized "Zambia in Full Color," he would not show his slides on Sunday! (He said something about a protest against "the way movies and slides are taking the place of preaching the Gospel in the churches.")

He stubbornly refused to be dissuaded. Any other day of the week, he said, but *never on Sunday!*

His final answer was: "The decision is mine to make — not yours!"

I was burning. "A legalist! They've sent me an anti-everything legalist."

As we talked that evening, I told him about some of the exciting things that had happened, about the small groups, and how we go about winning people and trying to build them up in the faith. I could see he was more skeptical of us than ever. The strain between us was increasing.

He excused himself and went to bed about eight o'clock.

Next morning (Sunday), as I was leaving to unlock the church about 8 a.m., he stopped me.

"I've got to talk to you," he said. "I don't think I should preach for you this morning. You aren't going to like what I have to say."

"What are you going to say?" I asked.

"That the richest church in history is doing practically nothing about a lost world. That there isn't any excuse for any church, even a pioneer church, not to give to reach the lost world."

"All that needs to be said," I answered. "The thing of which I'm afraid is that you are going to get up in the pulpit and harp about at lot of 'externals,' and try to put people 'under the law' on standards of dress and that kind of foolishness. In fact, I've been scared to death of you ever since you announced you wouldn't show those slides!"

[7] Romans 11:33

"And I've been scared of you!" he retorted. "I'd rather preach. But if you want, I'll just leave and get out of your way."

"I'll pray about it. I'll be back in about fifteen minutes, and I'll give you my answer then."

Carl was at the church. I laid my problem before him. His counsel was, "I think the spirit of your people will come through to him."

The Spirit seemed to say, "If this man can, by preaching one sermon, destroy what it has taken six years to build, it wasn't built very well anyway! And you'd better find out now."

"I can trust the Lord with you," I told the missionary. "Go ahead and preach."

I prayed. And kept praying. I prayed an unusual number of times in that service and with unusual earnestness. But I had a strange peace about the whole thing.

When he preached, it was *right on target.* It hit home with sharpness and spiritual power. He preached the truth and our sensitive people responded to his message.

When the "faith-promises" were counted, we had corporately trusted the Lord for $2,500 to build a building for a new black church in South Africa. I would have been excited if it had been $250.

And because of all our doubts and fears and lack of planning — no one could take the credit. The Spirit had done a significant thing among us. God had started us toward missionary-mindedness and had done it so differently and so much more beautifully than *we* could ever have planned or programmed it.

A side-benefit was that the missionary and I had been so honest with each other that, even though we were on opposite sides of many questions, we actually found a deep level of genuine fellowship in Christ.

Leadership Training

Paul gave Timothy instructions about training leaders in the early church:

> "The things that thou hast heard of me among many witnesses, the same commit thou to faithful men, who shall be able to teach others also" (2 Timothy 2:2).

This parallels Jesus' own "leadership training program":

Step 1: Gather a few men.
Step 2: Live with them (so they can see you as you are).
Step 3: Pour your life into them.
Step 4: Teach them all you know. (As they are ready for it, they'll let you know by *asking*. And the Spirit will also let you know.)
Step 5: Show them how.
Step 6: Let them learn by experience (even by failure).

Like nearly everything else at Our Heritage, "leadership training" is a very "loose" thing. We have purposely put ourselves into a position where, *if the Lord doesn't help us, we are going to be in trouble.*

There is no "program" of leadership training, as a separate entity. But leaders are being trained, nonetheless. Three components make up the training of leaders.

First, they are exposed to a teaching-type pulpit ministry.

It has been a difficult transition from the simplistic, flashy evangelistic preaching that characterized my Sunday morning ministry before. In those days, I seemed to have leaders a-plenty, but they had all the wrong reasons for wanting to lead.

It has been a costly transition.

It has been harder work. A lot of "junk" in my personal schedule has had to be dropped in order to have time for study and personal preparation.

But now, my whole congregation is having "committed to them" the things that are needed in the spiritual lives of leaders in God's church.

Second, there is an effort to involve all Christians in small groups.

There they learn how (taught by the Body, the Holy Spirit and the Word) to share life, to share Bible study, to share prayer and to share the challenge of outreach, witnessing and loving service. These are things that train leaders to be leaders in the living church.

Some groups are leaderless. The whole group leads, depending on the Spirit and the fellowship. And as this mutual ministry is carried on, the Spirit brings to the surface those who have been given gifts of leadership. In the natural course of group life, we discover the Spirit's choice of teachers, helpers, discerners, gifts of faith, knowledge (insight), wisdom (wise counsel), etc. Those with these gifts emerge, and the Spirit usually puts them to work immediately in the context of the group.

When the congregation as a whole has a need for leadership, we already know who to ask. Or, sometimes they have already volunteered.

Some groups pass the leadership around. This becomes a subtle form of on-the-job training.

Whether with a leader or leaderless, the purpose of the group is the same: that is, that the Holy Spirit be allowed freedom, in all the gatherings of the group and in its life between gatherings, to bring to the surface the gifts of leadership and grace. The group meetings are loose. The members spend a lot of time together. They wander freely from the Bible text into areas of concern. Plenty of freedom is allowed for group members to minister to one another.

In the groups, people are learning to walk in dependence on the Spirit and the Body. They are learning to be led by the Spirit. They are learning not to wait until they are elected to some church "position," but to find for themselves the Spirit's work for them. They are learning, without being told, what the "priesthood of believers" [8] and the "ministry of reconciliation" [9] are.

Third, there is a special kind of men's group with which I've been experimenting, seeking to stimulate Jesus' program of training.

For a part of this past year, I met weekly with a group of three or four men at a mealtime, in a restaurant. I would have welcomed more time together, but this is how the Spirit put them together. We spend about two hours a week together.

I shared my life with these men, more deeply than with any others with whom I meet. Problems. Hang-ups. Failures. As

[8] 1 Peter 2:5, 9
[9] 2 Corinthians 5:18

well as what the Lord had taught me. My purpose was to pour my life into them. To teach them all I know about Jesus Christ and His way. To answer their questions, deal with their hang-ups, fears and sins (even pointing them out, occasionally).

I was pleased with the results, even over the period of just a few months. As time went by, they began to volunteer for various jobs connected with the work in Scottsdale. They asked me to show them how to share their faith with others. And they began to bear fruit. I gave them various assignments involving church nitty-gritty, visitation, sharing their testimony in public, representing me at meetings, etc. It seemed to me they grew spiritually and became ready to lead much more rapidly than usual. And, again and again, they ministered to me in my personal spiritual needs.

It's an experiment I intend to continue and to expand.[10]

The keys to development of spiritual leadership – leadership that is of the Spirit – are:

1. Selection of people by the Spirit.
2. The Spirit gives gifts to them of what is needed in order for them to lead in the church.
3. These gifts are discovered in the context of sharing in small group situations and in the congregation.

Youth Ministry

We do not have a traditional "youth program." We prefer to call it a "ministry."

The most well-attended youth meeting is a Bible study. They call it "Bible Rap."[11] It is composed of contemporary singing, a taught Bible study, small group sharing and conversational prayer, and just being together. It meets at "Ron's house" on Tuesday nights.

There is no rigid set of "no-no's" to confine their activities to things comfortably acceptable to the adults in the church.

They dress as they please. "Grubbies," slacks, shorts, minis,

[10] For more about this plan, see Robert Coleman's book *The Master Plan of Evangelism,* published by Fleming H. Revell.

[11] A "rap" is a talk session.

maxis, bare feet, sandals, long hair, short hair – it's not an issue.

The issue is the Living Person of Jesus and His Word.

Social programs are incidental. Whenever they are together, they are "in the Word." They'd rather pray than play.

Let me illustrate with a description of two recent "parties" held by the church's young people.

The first was a surprise "birthday party." After the guest of honor arrived at the house, a basin of water was produced, and after appropriate Scriptural exposition by a youthful leader, they washed one another's feet as an act of love. They gathered in a circle to pray for the guest of honor. They prayed for a long time, because so many teenagers wanted to share in prayer. The "birthday party" closed with a celebration of the Lord's Supper. One previously unconverted young person prayed that night to receive Christ.

Then there was the "going away party" for a young man who had just been drafted. It was an hour-long testimony meeting in which about two dozen young people and adults thanked God publicly for how He had used "Jack" in their lives. A few gospel folk songs were sung. And, again, before cake and punch were served, all prayed for the young draftee.

I watch with open-mouthed awe at the spontaneous revolution taking place – wondering, sometimes, if I might not be dreaming the whole thing.

Not all parents, not all young people like this totally "spiritual" emphasis. But "Ron" feels it is what the church of Jesus Christ is all about – even for teens. I agree.

Several small groups (called "action groups"), some meeting on high school campuses and some in homes, give opportunity for close-knit fellowship and encourage daily witnessing.

Two "master action groups" provide deeper fellowship and training for the young leaders of these groups.

Students are led to Christ by other students in the cafeteria, in the library, between classes, and after school. Essays, papers and speeches prepared for class presentation become "tracts" and "sermons" telling the reality of the Living Jesus.

One teenager was all excited as she told me, "I'm a great-grandmother! I led Cindy to Jesus. Cindy led Carol to Jesus. And now Carol has led Debbie to Jesus. I'm a great-grandmother!"

They sing the love of Christ to the beat of the now generation – their generation. Folk music and gospel rock combine with majestic old hymns and "traditional" songs as they praise God in a way that speaks to them and their peers.

Ken Strawn, a layman with a love for "their kind of music," has brought together about thirty teenage voices in a group called "His People." It's the nearest thing we have to a "youth program." Electronic guitars, tamborines, and drums accentuate the sound of music to the glory of the Lord. It's very contemporary. It's a little "rocky." It speaks for their generation – for them.

At least once a month, the Sunday morning meeting rocks with their joyful singing and playing. And the congregation says "Amen!" with their hands, in grateful *applause*.

The music and the reality of the Living Jesus we share in common with them accounts, in part, for the fact that it is not unusual for teenagers and collegians to comprise a third or more of the Sunday morning congregation.

The youth ministry took this direction while Carl Jackson was serving as youth director. He did a great deal of experimenting and spent hours upon hours just talking with teenagers.

Every "canned" program he tried seemed to fall flat. The kids weren't interested, and who could blame them?

So, he began just spending time with them. *Personal* time. Doing nothing much but "rapping." His office was always full of teenagers telling him their troubles. Praying with him. He was never too busy to talk. Nothing was more important than any teenager who just wanted to talk.

He kept experimenting and waiting on the Spirit. And, in every experiment, the Holy Spirit seemed to lead him in one direction: away from youth "services," "canned" meetings, heavy preparation, lots of social activities, and a lot of other things that characterize the "traditional church youth program."

He stopped programming for the church's kids who did not seem to care about a really vital life with Jesus and began concentrating almost entirely on those who would respond to something really spiritual.

He was available to the former. They were always invited to the meetings. But the ministry was geared to learning how to make Christ everything in life. Simple Bible study, conversational prayer (as long and as often as they wanted to pray) and training in personal evangelism became "the program."

The group immediately became smaller. But out of that group came a significant number who sensed a call to full time Christian service and a constant stream of kids who openly shared their faith on campus.

Now, under the leadership of a home-grown director, a young "long-hair" named Ron Rogers, the extent of person-to-person ministry to youth has increased. He now has nearly complete freedom from anything that would make his ministry less than completely person-centered. He has only one job to do: win and build young people in the Lord Jesus Christ.

Until very recently, the youth ministry has always been a part-time thing. But it has been effective in producing "live" young Christians, simply because there has always been someone willing to take the time and to make the personal sacrifice to be available to young people day and night.

I think it is evident that this is not really a program. Just a man pouring his life into the lives of young people. A man to whom Jesus Christ is living reality and to whom teenagers are worth dying for.

Our youth ministry is not "ideal" in my personal view. I believe the ideal is for teenagers to be completely integrated into the total life of the church.

There is no "generation gap" in Christ.[12] The church should not recognize one. Older teenagers are, in reality, young adults. And, as such, they can make a significant contribution at every level of church life.

Today's young people more readily accept change. They are interested in something real. They will unceremoniously turn off anything phony. They seem more ready to give themselves, all

[12] Colossians 3:11, Galatians 3:28, 1 Corinthians 12:13

their energy, and their very lives in the unconditional way demanded by Jesus.

The church needs them in its mainstream, and needs them badly. And they need the church, the whole church, and the ministry of all its members.

In the future, Lord willing, there will be less and less distinction between youth ministry and general Body life, with its mutual ministry that recognizes no gap between the generations.

XIII

BUT WHAT ABOUT OLD WINESKINS?

I AM gratefully aware that Our Heritage has had one great advantage over most evangelical churches. This advantage has tended to give us greater freedom as we have moved ahead with restructuring the church. That is the fact that Our Heritage is a new church built almost entirely around people won to Christ through its own ministry.

At the time we began preaching renewal, clearing superfluous meetings from the schedule, and forming small groups, *ninety percent* of the members of the church were *brand new Christians,* "untainted" by experience with traditional evangelicalism.

Many had come to Christ out of non-evangelical church backgrounds, and a few institutional church barnacles were still hanging on them. Also, they'd had a short period of exposure to a pre-renewal Our Heritage. They had tasted "the glorious evangelical status quo."[1] These factors accounted, in part, for the opposition which led to the "Exodus of '69."[2]

But "old Christians," the "dyed-in-the-wool" kind, or the "hard-shell" kind we did not have.

Those who were already born-again Christians when they came to us made up no more than ten percent of the church. And those the Lord had given us were people as hungry for renewal and as open for change as we were. They were among the first to accept the "renewal theology" we began to preach.

[1] See Chapters 1 and 2.
[2] Chapter 7.

I'm no hero. I'm the kind of a pastor who "resigns" (to his wife) three times a week – every time a sticky problem comes up. Had the Lord not given me a group of people more likely to respond to new ideas, I'd have probably been last seen three years ago heading East with my clerical tail between my legs!

God knew me and He knew the people. And knowing what He wanted to build here, He put us together. It's been the most exciting experience of my life.

However, I firmly believe that many of the changes I have been telling about *can take place in many older, more "traditional" churches.*

In the first place, wherever there are true believers in Jesus, the Spirit of God is already working. These believers may be involved in the kind of church structure that stifles the sharing of life in Christ together, and inhibits spiritual growth. They may be all entangled in the red tape of the ecclesiastical bureaucracy that exists in many denominations. They may have prejudices, wrong ideas, and know nothing of dependence on the Spirit in any kind of practical, day-by-day way. They may seem to be almost mummified in the grave dressings of unbiblical church tradition. They may be opposed to anything that would disturb the status quo. But that doesn't alter the fact that if they have thrown themselves on Christ for salvation and He lives in them, they are a part of the Body of Christ.

They cannot just be "written off"!

We must *not* fit their mold, or pamper them in their immaturity, or back down in the face of their carnal outbursts. We must not stop seeking to bring renewal and revival to the church just because they don't like it.

But neither can we just write them off. They are brothers and sisters. Jesus said, if we do not have love for them, the world has a right to come to the conclusion that we are really not Christians at all. [3]

For these reasons, those who want to see church renewal cannot just "forget" the institutional church. The people of God are

[3] John 13:35

there. The Spirit is there, in the people. I *need* those brothers and sisters very much. And they need me.

I may be committed to tearing down the old man-made traditions and trying to replace institutionalism with something better, but I dare not be committed to forsaking my fellow members of the Body of Christ. Or to belittling in any way what the Spirit is doing in and through them. How can I? I share with them the *same Body* and the *same Life.*

It is always easier to tell another pastor how to do it, when you aren't in his boots. Just like it is easier to "raise" other people's children. But I have been asked by a number of people *how I would start, if I were seeking to spark renewal in an old, established church.*

First, I would seek personal renewal.

It is quite useless for a pastor or lay leader talking about reviving or renewing the church, if he himself is not a candidate for revival and renewal. It's as silly as that old parental formula for certain failure: "Do as I say, not as I do."

Renewal principles cannot merely be *taught,* they must be *caught* from one experiencing new life. You cannot set me afire by merely showing me a picture of a flame. You must put me in contact with the real thing.

When a man is sick enough of the death in the church; the empty shame of much of its accepted routine; the powerlessness of its agencies, auxiliaries and programs to fulfill its mission in the world; the foolishness of its actual goals; the disaster of its divisiveness; the fruitlessness of its dependence on human strength, influence, and means; and when he is willing to accept the blame for the church being as it is — he is a candidate for renewal.

When a man comes to realize that all that is wrong with the church as it has been handed to him, is wrong because of the very kinds of things that are wrong in his own personal life and ministry; and he is beginning to be honest enough to admit that the greatest roadblock to renewal is "number one" — he is a candidate for renewal.

When a man sees that God's plan calls for something better than what the church is and what it is experiencing as he knows it; and when he is so hungry for that "something better" that he cannot possibly be satisfied any longer with the decaying status quo — he is a candidate for renewal.

When that sickness over the church's death, that realization that he is part of the problem, that hunger for God's "something better," gets *so bad* that the man is willing to pay *whatever price is necessary* to get new life for himself and for his church; and he aches so deeply for spiritual reality that he is *willing to die trying to get it* — he is a candidate for renewal.

And, finally, when the man's illusions about his ability to do anything at all about the situation in his own life, or that of the church, all seem to be lying in a heap of useless rubble before his eyes; he sees himself as nothing, his talents and education and experience as of no value, his ideas and influence as zero; he sees the only hope for renewal and life in himself and the church as resting solely on God the Father, Son and Holy Spirit — that man is a candidate for renewal.

Before the teachings of the Word of God, a man must ask himself what he is called to do, what the church is supposed to be, and why he and it are not fulfilling those callings.

And he must ask from what resources God expects those callings to be fulfilled.

The Word has the answer:

> "Faithful is He that calleth you, who also (Himself) will do it" (1 Thessalonians 5:24).
>
> "Not by (human) might, nor by (human) strength, but by my Spirit, saith the Lord" (Zechariah 4:6).
>
> "Without me (Christ) you can do nothing" (John 15:5).
>
> "He which hath begun a good work in you will perform it until the day of Jesus Christ" (Philippians 1:6).
>
> "It is God that worketh in you, both to will and to do of His good pleasure" (Philippians 2:13).
>
> "I can do all things through Christ which strengtheneth me" (Philippians 4:13).
>
> "The just shall live (walk, work, minister, etc.) by faith" (Romans 1:17).

All that is death and stagnation in the church is a result of *man's efforts* – even his efforts to serve God. Life and wholeness in the church can never come by simply re-directing human efforts. Life and wholeness are only found in God Himself, His Son and His Spirit.

Man must get out of the way, resign, quit, give up – and make room in his program for God to operate as Head and Life-source of the church.

The first person who must "let go and let God" is the pastor or layman who sees the need for renewal. That person's *personal renewal* is the first step to renewal in any church.

Second, I would begin immediately to preach renewal.

I would ask the Spirit to renew my pulpit ministry.

I would begin to *teach*. I would begin to teach a theology of renewal. I would find my source of this "new" theology in the teachings of the *New Testament* about the church.

Even if it cut squarely across my denominational loyalties and I found it saying some things contrary to what my contemporaries were saying, I would begin to preach and teach the *New Testament Church*. I would declare: "It can happen again, *now!*"

Sermons would describe how the Body functioned in *The Acts*, *First Corinthians* 12-14, and *Ephesians* 4. It would be pointed out how we fall short of functioning effectively as the Body, today. Care would be taken to spotlight what there is in church structure as it now exists that prevents the New Testament fellowship and mutual ministry.

I would preach the priesthood of all believers.

The responsibility of the family to serve as a unit of spiritual growth and witness would be stressed as a key to sparking renewal.

Evangelistic sermons would be laid aside to concentrate on building disciples out of the believers the church already had. I would make clear the plan of salvation, and perhaps even give invitations (if that was the usual pattern for that church), but my preaching would be aimed at the ignorance and immaturity of the saints.

I would preach the Resurrection of Jesus, again and again and again. From the Scriptures and personal experience, I would seek to show what it means to the Christian that Jesus is alive in the Christian.

The distinction between what is of the flesh and what is of the Spirit would be spotlighted. I would seek to understand this distinction for my own life and ministry and then I would share what I had learned.

I would teach absolute dependence on the Spirit in all situations and for all needs. And I would seek to practice it.

Honesty would become a keynote in my pulpit ministry. I would ask for courage and grace to admit my failures, my doubts, my struggle with the flesh. I would seek to be real and practical in my preaching and teaching.

I would preach love and then admit that I did not have it myself and needed the help of other Christians in finding it.

I would preach grace. I would seek to stop preaching law or trying to build the church on the basis of law.

I would dare to dream of the ideal church, in the light of the New Testament. Then I would share those dreams with the congregation, showing what changes would be necessary to reach them.

As long as I have been a pastor, no one has ever told me what to preach. I have had freedom to say what I felt from the pulpit. Most evangelical pastors enjoy that freedom. I would take advantage of that freedom. I would take advantage of that freedom to preach the theology of renewal.

Third, I would work with the church board.

I would continually seek the leadership of the Holy Spirit as to what steps to take and when. I would go as far toward renewal with them as the Spirit and their responsiveness would allow.

At a weekend retreat[4] for board members and their wives, renewal concepts could be taught and discussed. They could be introduced to a small group experience, and be given opportunity to relate on a personal level with one another.

[4] See, *A New Face for the Church,* Lawrence O. Richards, Zondervan, pp. 167-170 for a complete suggested retreat program.

If retreat does not seem to be the thing to do, an evening "briefing" can feature some of these things. Simply to go through the "Quaker Questions" [5] with the board would help to create a warmer, more understanding, more personal atmosphere among the members.

Depending upon their willingness, one could let the first hour of every board meeting become a "small group" experience, involving sharing and prayer on a personal level.

Officially, I would seek to get the board involved in evaluating the church as it is for the purpose of setting non-numerical goals.[6] This would be a practical step toward getting the eyes of church leaders away from nickles and noses and on the really top priority business of the Body of Christ.

I would concentrate on a few responsive members of the board. Get close to them. Not for "political" purposes but to share life in Christ with them, to be ministered to by them, and to discover soul-fellowship. Perhaps two or three would meet weekly for that purpose.[7]

Fourth, whether I got to first base with the leaders or not, I would start a small group.

I would not even try it with old Christians who are satisfied with the status quo in their own lives or in the church, or who "already know it all." That's the shortest route to frustration and disappointment I know.

I would start with (1) non-Christians, (2) new Christians, (3) weak Christians who recognize that they are weak, or (4) really Spirit-minded Christians who are honest with themselves, or want to be.

I would not try to kill any giants. I would work with whomever is positive toward renewal. I would leave to the Spirit those who are negative. I would not try to convince them against their will or force them into a group. It would not work anyway.

[5] Chapter 10, p. 145.

[6] See *A New Face for the Church*, pp. 194-205, for a very workable evaluation survey leading toward the setting of such goals.

[7] Robert Coleman has written an excellent book about building disciples by working with a small number of men, *The Master Plan of Evangelism*, Revell.

If I could find *one couple* (or, even just one *person*) besides my wife and me who was willing to be open and really wanted to get to know Christ better and to experience real soul-fellowship in Him, I would start a "little church" with that. If more would respond, fine. If not, praise God for one.

It does not matter whether that couple has influence in the church or not. (Perhaps they are not even "saved.") The renewal we desire is not dependent on "influence" or "power." The Spirit can start His renewal there – with two or three gathered in Jesus' name. And it will grow like yeast in a lump of dough.

Fifth, I would do everything I could to get members involved with each other on a personal spiritual level.

I would ask God to help *me* to stop holding people off at arm's length. *I would place people above programs on my personal priority list.*

I would give midweek service attenders (perhaps even Sunday nighters) a taste of face-to-face small group life – a taste of the priesthood of believers. Perhaps, instead of preaching, I would try giving in brief the background of a Scripture passage, and then divide the congregation into groups of twelve or less, to share how the passage relates to their lives, and then to pray specifically for one another. Guideline questions could be given each group, if this seemed necessary.

Wherever it was possible, opportunities would be provided for person-to-person sharing: Sunday school class, existing men's and women's groups – even during the Sunday morning service.

(As the Spirit leads.)

Sixth, I would wait patiently for the Lord.

I would hang loose, depend on the Spirit, and trust His timing.

I would ask for grace to keep from trying to *force* renewal. I would seek to trust the Spirit and then *let it happen.*

I cannot renew anything. I cannot bring new life to a dead church. Only He who had the power to raise Christ from the dead can do that.

I will wait, patiently, for the Lord.

He won't fail.

As I wait for Him, I will thank Him for every heartbreaking

problem along the road to renewal, every failure, every crushing defeat, every weakening of my position or tarnishing of my "image," and every evidence of my dispensability, every time He proves again that He can do it without me. For these "blessings" are the chisels of the Master Sculptor, reshaping me, so that I will fit and be useful in His renewed church.

XIV

LIVING CIRCLE

SIX YEARS ago, when we came to open the doors of this new church, we carried in our minds a dream of the kind of church it would be. Part of that dream was that it would *reproduce itself at least every five years.*

Nothing was done in the way of scheming and maneuvering to make this happen. It was just a dream. A hope. A back-of-the-mind idea. After we began moving toward new life as a church, it seemed to be shoved to the burners farthest back and was not a key thought at all. It was one of that multitude of things newly trusted to the Lord and all but forgotten.

But God hadn't forgotten the desires of our hearts. [1]

Just five years and five months from our own "presentation Sunday," a new congregation began meeting. Its nucleus was people from Our Heritage. Our Heritage was its "mother church."

Circle Wesleyan Church. Usually referred to as simply "Circle Church." Carl Jackson, our former associate pastor, who was so positively influential in the changes that have taken place at Our Heritage, was its "pioneer pastor."

But the new congregation is not very similar to the way I would have described my dream of five years before.

Come and see.

It is Sunday morning, about 9:35. We have arrived about ten minutes early at the elementary school cafetorium, which is the

[1] Psalm 37:4.

meeting place of Circle Church. Carl and Ann Jackson are there along with a layman and his wife. They are busily arranging about sixty folding chairs in a double circle. Hymn books and New Testaments (*Good News for Modern Man,* published by the American Bible Society) are placed on alternating chairs. Ann starts the electric coffee maker. (Everything needed for today's meeting except chairs and piano has to be carried in and out each Sunday.) The men roll the school's spinet piano into position.

By now the families who make up the congregation are beginning to gather. Their unusually friendly chatter is the prelude to worship. Typically, the second row of seats fills up first. Whole families sit together. Only the tiniest tots are taken to an adjacent room that serves as a nursery.

At 9:45 the meeting begins. An air of expectancy is evident as we look across the circle into the faces of the people with whom we share this time.

If you have not been here before, you do not know where to expect the leader of the meeting to be seated. There is no lectern or pulpit. No platform. Not even a break in the circle prominent enough to set the pastor's folding chair apart from the others.

Today, the meeting begins with prayer. Last week a song opened it. Next week it may begin another way. We have been given "worship folders," but they contain no rigid "order of service," only a series of brief statements explaining the significance of the various parts of the meeting as it is planned today.

Except for its fundamental informality and the pervading unmistakable recognition on the part of the congregation that Christ is really there, this meeting has many of the elements that make up the worship services of most churches.

They sing solid old hymns and gospel songs from the hymnal. A mimeographed sheet carries the words of a few joyful, positive choruses and songs not contained in the hymnal.

The Scripture is read from the circle by a pre-selected layman. It's one of the Psalms.

Prayer, too, is informal. Several members of the group lead in prayer in very conversational tones. There is not a sign of "King James English" in any of the prayers. Several very personal petitions are included for members in the group.

Carl, from his seat in the circle, mentions the fact that there is an offering plate in the rear for giving "as the Spirit leads." No offering will be taken.

The announcements concern the time and location of a new "Living Circle" (home group) to be started this week, plus mention of the list of existing groups contained in the worship folder. We glance at the list and find that about a dozen "Living Circles" will meet in a dozen homes this week. There are no other meetings scheduled. No Sunday evening service (two or three of the "circles" meet on Sunday night). No midweek prayer meeting. No committee meetings. No Women's Society. No clubs. No choir practice. Just "Living Circles."

In introducing the brief "Share Time" in the worship service, Carl suggests that a few people share "what has happened the previous week that you can praise God for . . . even problems . . . not just neat little witnessing experiences, but anything God is using in your life."

The major part of the worship meeting is what Carl calls "Teaching." It is definitely the preaching of the Word – the sermon. But it is geared to the spiritual growth of the people who make up the Body. His preaching relates the reality of the Living Christ to the daily lives of the people. It contains instruction in the proper function of the Body. He begins today's message in a sitting position, open Bible in his lap. As he continues, he stands as he emphasizes certain points. The Word is carefully brought to bear on every thought. This marks the teaching with the stamp of authority.

During this part of the meeting, the impact of the circular seating begins to come through. You aren't looking at the backs of people's heads. You are looking into their faces. You can see the reaction of your fellow worshipers and sense how the Spirit is working as the teaching progresses. You are blessed yourself as you see visible signs of the blessing others are receiving. If something "registers" on the face of someone else, you, yourself, think again about what was said, lest you miss its significance for you.

The response of the listening congregation is only barely audible. But a quiet chuckle, a "yes, that's right" under-the-breath, a visible glisten in the eyes or a smile responds to the truth.

Even a negative response, and infrequently there are these, brings true feelings into the open and shares them with a loving, accepting fellowship.

This meeting may or may not include "special music." There is none today, and no one seems embarrassed about it. In fact, the worship service is always changing, as this young church experiments to find what most effectively brings the results they desire.

When the teaching is ended, it is time for what Circle Church knows as "The Share Fellowship."

The children and young people go to designated corners of the cafetorium where teachers wait to lead them in a sharing experience geared to their level of understanding. The Share Fellowship is not a Sunday school. The church purchases no published materials, though teachers of the children do use visual aids. The entire children's section of The Share Fellowship has studied *The Gospel of John*. A Bible lesson is taught, briefly, but the emphasis is on *sharing*. Teachers guide the children to sharing with the class their problems and things that are important to them. Then they pray about these things together. All are taught "conversational" prayer. Often the teacher will make prayer assignments. That is, he will ask one child to pray during the coming week for the shared problem of another. Then the next Sunday they will talk about what has happened – what God has done in answer to prayer.

When the worship portion of the meeting is over, the adults head for the coffee maker, and then, cups in hand, return to the circle for Adult Share Fellowship.

Discussion there primarily revolves around the pastor's teaching. At least it begins there. Sometimes Carl corners a layman before worship service and asks him to try to find something in the sermon on which to comment or raise a question. This serves as a catalyst for discussion. Today, someone in the group has a question about one of the pastor's points. Carl spends a moment or two clarifying what he meant. A housewife across the circle relates the point to something that happened between her and a neighbor this week. A young engineer asks a related question, pulling in a problem in his relationship with a man with whom he works. Even a visitor, here for the first time, enters the discussion with an unusually perceptive statement. There is freedom to sidetrack to things that are of vital concern and to share how God is working.

It is not unusual for a problem or an experience to be shared that is deep enough to be shared with tears. Here is a real fellowship of real people sharing their real lives together so that their faith in Christ is able to come to grips with life's realities.

Because this new church is being built, not only of evangelical Christians who know and believe the Bible's basic doctrines, but also of the unchurched and people from non-evangelical churches, sometimes what is shared in the Share Fellowship is based on *wrong doctrine.*

I asked Carl about this problem. He explained the church's approach to it: "The approach we try to take on these things is not 'Now listen, brother, we'd better get this straightened out right now.' Our approach is to let them say what they want to say, and not to affront them or condemn their 'belief.' Many of them came from churches which have not taught the Bible as being the whole counsel of God, so they may have a lot of confusion. If we were to turn on them and attack every little error in their thinking, they are going to resent it. So, we just patiently work with them. We may even seem to be 'compromising' for a while, because we don't condemn them for their error. We let them say what they will. I have discovered that I don't have to convince them. *The Spirit convinces men of the truth.*"

While they are saying "what they will," of course, Carl is teaching them the truth Sunday after Sunday, and they are studying the Bible (many, for the first time in their lives), in "Living Circles" in an atmosphere of openness to one another and to the Spirit and the truth. And soon, they are saying "what they will," but what they are saying is the same as what the Bible is saying. The Spirit has faithfully done His promised work.[2]

Ninety minutes after the opening of worship, the Share Fellowship ends. We leave with a sense that we have been involved in something today that is *alive*. We have been touched by something *real*. There is an inescapable sense that God is still involved in the lives of men and women, and we have just witnessed a glimpse of His working.

We are not "impressed" with the beauty of the sanctuary, the perfection of the finely executed service, the splendor of the music, the size of the crowd, nor even the skillfulness of the oratory we have heard. For none of those things have been "the point" today. But we have met a group of people – *really* met them – who have helped us to see past human instruments to view afresh *the God who is there*.

During the week these people gather in one another's homes for small group meetings called "Living Circles."

The Living Circles are Bible study groups. The sharing of life that characterizes the Sunday morning Share Fellowship continues to open up as the people, in small groups, bring their lives to the Word of God and are willing to expose themselves to one another in its light.

The Body of Christ becomes a real thing, whose personal ministry is needed from week to week.

"As long as there is an attitude of openness," declares the pastor, "people share deeply their lives, their problems, their questions. It's got to be 'I accept you for who you are, regardless of what you think, and regardless of your level of spirituality. You may be very different from me. You may manifest gifts of the Spirit that I don't manifest, but you are one with me in Christ, so we're going to learn from each other.' "

In the Living Circles, the people begin to learn that the Spirit of God ministers to each one through the others. "The Spirit of God in you ministers to the Spirit of God in me." Together, through this mutuality of ministry they are instructed. The group begins to experience the flow of the Life of Christ. Reticent mem-

[2] John 16:13

bers begin to feel confident enough to share what really hurts them.

It soon becomes apparent that those who go through deep trouble saying nothing about it in the Body actually suffer more than those who take the Body with them through their struggles, and thus have the prayers and encouragement of the Body as they go through it. Often the Body's involvement comes, not from the sharing of every gruesome detail of a problem, but in the simple admission, "I've got a problem and I want you to pray for me" — an admission that says, "I need the Body of Christ." Then, the rest of the Body, its weaker and stronger members, begin to minister and to pray.

As visible miracles happen in the lives of those who have shared, the more retiring members of the group are emboldened to share their problems. The Body ministry snowballs. And it's beautiful.

It has taken time for mutual trust and confidence to be built to the point where this kind of Body ministry can operate at a really effective level. But just *weeks* after the beginning of the church fellowship, exciting results were being reported from the groups.

Evangelism is taking place in and through the groups. Presently there are nearly twice as many adults involved in Living Circles as in the congregation's Sunday morning meeting. Members of the groups who previously thought sharing their faith was "out of place" in their professions now share Christ openly.

I asked Carl why he thought this was happening.

"The small group has built a personal confidence in the reality of Christ. The members have really come to see Christ as He is. They see Him as a loving Christ, not a Christ who teaches a lot of prohibitions. They come to see the relationship with Him as a very positive thing in their lives. And their witness comes as something natural, positive, confident and spontaneous."

Living Circles are scattered broadly over the metropolitan area. Most have been formed on a geographical basis. Though the church is only a few months old, it is already considering "mothering" new congregations in some of these localities.

When ten or twelve people are involved in a Living Circle, consideration is given to the formation of another group using two or three couples from the old group as a nucleus for the new one.

Carl sees the ideal size of the congregation as under one hundred. From the viewpoint of the involvement in the Share Fellowship and the economics of big buildings, he feels a larger congregation could defeat the purpose of the church. Instead of trying to build one "super church," he envisions his future ministry as that of a sort of "circuit-ridin' pastor-teacher," with three or four small congregations meeting at different times on Sunday. Laymen would be taught and trusted to handle all church affairs and the church "program," which consists entirely of the mutual ministry of small groups.

Social involvement, outreach, evangelism and other programs of outward ministry are expected to flow from the Holy Spirit's living ministry in the congregation and the groups.

From before the first meeting of Circle Church, the community has been told that buildings and programs would play second fiddle to people in the new church.

If it were possible to rent facilities indefinitely, a building would probably never be built. If it becomes necessary to build, simplicity, economy and multiplicity of function will be keynotes of it.

The feeling of the pastor and congregation is that, unless it is kept in perspective as a purely utilitarian thing, a building can become a little stone god to worship, slave for and depend upon. They feel that nothing, in the church of Jesus Christ, must detract from His Lordship and His personal ministry in and through His people.

The rented school cafeteria has been far from perfect. But God has used its imperfections to draw attention and trust to His Person. Food on the floor isn't as lovely as soft carpet, but it is so *un*lovely that the fellowship looks beyond it to the loveliness of Christ.

Holy Communion is served from the only available table, a rickety, grubby, ugly little four legged furniture-maker's nightmare. Against such a backdrop the sacrifice and living communion of Christ are all that takes the congregation's attention. None may revel in the beauty of the communion table.

For several weeks, the school failed to provide a piano, as agreed. At first there was resentment, discomfort at this new "adjustment." Then, pastor and people began to realize that God was trying to teach them something deeper about the Body of Christ and the fact that their only real need was to worship *Him*. And simply because they did not have a piano, worship became more meaningful than ever. The people sang better. God became more real in their gathering together.

Circle Church is a new congregation still measuring its life in months, many of its people new to evangelicalism and to acceptance of the Bible as the final and reliable authority in faith in life. And yet, the signs of vital New Testament Life are there. Not perfected. Not in mature form. But the signs of Life are there. Its character carries the stamp of mutual ministry.

Here are a people who walk in openness and fellowship with one another.

Evangelism is taking place, softly, gently, with no pressure of any kind . . . real evangelism.

Families have time to live together. Individuals have time for community involvement and neighborhood witness.

There is an expectation of the supernatural. They believe in miracles.

There is a constantly deepening awareness of the need for total surrender to God.

They see God as a loving God. They see Him not as a God who is "out to get us," but as a God who wants to give us all He has.

Christ is real to them. They share what He is doing week by week. All have opportunity to see Him alive and working.

Wherever two or three of them get together the conversation turns almost immediately to Christ and what He is doing.

They love each other. It is not uncommon for these people to tell one another they love each other.

They feed constantly on the Word. There is an unusual openness to it. They study it not only in the groups, but also in their families.

They are a people who are learning to trust God with the "little" things of life as well as with the "big" things. They are learning to see God in *everything that happens.*

"This is not a fast way to build a church," says Carl, "but it is a solid way to build a *fellowship.* . . . It's the most exciting thing I've ever been involved in in my life!"

It's a Living Circle. Never stagnant. Ever growing. Ever reaching out. An ever-widening circle touching more and more lives. But, most important, in touch with *the Life.*

XV

"MEANWHILE, BACK AT THE CHURCH"

In my most brazen and wild-eyed surges of renewal passion, I have cried for the Lord to sweep away our buildings and land, and to miraculously reduce us to a scattered aggregation of "little churches" meeting in homes – home churches, each completely free to *be* the church in its fullest sense. Autonomous, little, local organs in the Body of Christ, dependent only on the Spirit, the Word, and their own mutual ministry. Groups of families, too small and too alive to struggle and sweat to form such ineffective agencies of pseudo-spiritual worth as Sunday school, youth group, church board, finance committee and commission on evangelism.

Is it even really possible to be free to be all God wants His Church to be as long as we continue to be an "institution" which can be thought of as a pointed building at 4640 North Granite Reef Road?

In my most sane moments, I have admitted that having or not having a building is not really the issue. People and their attitudes, what people are depending on, what people are looking for when they come together, and what people share when they come together are the issue.

In my most honest moments, I have had to admit that none of the changes that have taken place in our fellowship have come without the Holy Spirit having to overcome *my own* resistance to change. While boasting loudly of my "progressive" attitude and desire for renewal, a part of me has resisted the Spirit's inroads into territory I felt belonged to me. Even after surrendering to His will, I have often muscled back in and tried to do things my way.

He has done miracles. He has wrought whatever really beneficial changes have taken place at Our Heritage. Invariably *I* have tried to take the credit. (That is, when I wasn't asking if He really knew what He was doing.)

In spite of my resistance, vacillating, roadblocking, and unbelief, He has begun the renewal process. He has begun to press us to Himself – to shape us into His image.

He has *begun* . . .

No one *dare* claim it is any more than a beginning. The real daring will come in the years ahead.

It is really too soon to have written such a book as this. One might get the impression that we think we have experienced complete renewal and now are free from all our establishment hangups, so that the Holy Spirit now has complete, unhindered freedom to recreate the *Book of Acts* here in Scottsdale. That would be a false impression.

In just the last few weeks, we have been vividly confronted with graphic illustrations of the naked truth that, while progress has been made, both pastor and people here are no more than renewal infants, still constantly in need of more milk,[1] more spankings,[2] and many more changes.[3] We are just learning to walk. We still fall down a lot. We still would rather play than work. We have a terribly short attention span.

We still stick out our chubby little double chins and stubbornly insist, "I'd rather do it *myself!*" So God lets us. And then, when we finally admit that we can't, He patiently comes to our aid and uses our failure to remind us again of our commitment to "depend on the Spirit instead of the flesh."[4]

A recent board meeting spent three hours trying to attack the church's financial problems in the same old institutional ways,

[1] 1 Peter 2:2
[2] Hebrews 12:5-11
[3] 2 Corinthians 3:18
[4] Chapter 5

almost without any evidence of faith. We fell back on the tired old "get-'em-involved" technique, complete with the suggestion that the pastor lead the busy-work brigade, coupled with disparaging remarks about the doubtful quality of the commitment of "those *other* people" who were not deeply involved in the organizational machinery of the institution. There was almost a complete lack of reference to the "Seven Principles,"[5] and an alarming degree of intent to reverse the direction we have been traveling recently, to return to dependence on the good old human machine that has "worked so well in other churches."

Due to lack of clear direction, it was mostly talk and very little concrete action. Thank God. (The great immediate benefit[6] that came out of the meeting was that it showed up the need for a re-preaching of the basic New Testament principles of Body life, before the temptation to return to the old ways of law and death became a full-scale movement in that direction.)

I could pull my self-righteous robes about me on occasions such as this, and with a sickening air of superiority could look down my oversized nose at these lay leaders and humbly announce my martyrdom . . . if it weren't for one thing: I, myself, a thousand times, have toyed with the temptation to go back. Every time someone tells of the "great effectiveness" of some new program gimmick or evangelism technique that a sister church has used to increase its attendance or offerings, I have considered pulling off the shelf some of the old, discarded ideas, and pressing people into the organization to carry them out. I have faced the choice again and again whether or not to go back to making the institution the focal point of our lives and work and to begin driving for statistical increases again, even though it meant taking the old shortcuts that would mean the sacrifice of Christian liberty and spontaneity in the Spirit and consequent curtailment of the development of the Priesthood of all believers.

The "sifting process" still goes on. People still decide to leave because the church is not doing something for them they think it should be doing, or because the pastor is not functioning in

[5] Chapters 5 and 6
[6] Romans 8:28

the traditional way (i.e., calling on the members twice a year, etc.), or because the organization is "too loose," or because the church and pastor are not taking certain legalistic stands that have traditionally become part of evangelical churches.

And it still hurts when they leave.

When it happens, the old temptations come back to nag and haunt.

"Perhaps everyone else is right, and we are wrong. I mean, if we were right wouldn't we be adding hundreds to our church? Maybe it would be best after all to lighten things up. To *demand* the tithe. To lay down the law about 'involvement' in the machine. To dive deeply into programming again. To back off from being so personal. To beef up the church's dependence on the pastor. How about just one more big, flashy, exciting Sunday school contest?"

Just as I was trying to finish this chapter, I went through three weeks of that! The summer slump was upon us – numerically and financially. I was tired. Then a family called to say they were leaving the church for several of the above reasons. It was almost too much.

Satan got a foothold because of my resentment over this loss, and under satanic oppression I fought with God about all these things for three full weeks. So that, even after all He has shown us and all that we have seen of new life in the church, in my blindness I would have given it all up for a ten percent increase in church attendance and a credit balance on the books!

But once you've caught a glimpse of "God's Church" (even though experiencing it fully may still be future tense), to go back, to stop pressing for the full experience of His Life in the church is to *die*. I could not live with myself. It would be like denying the New Birth to return to the old way of life.

So, once again (and it probably will not be the last time), I have taken a fresh grip on the New Testament concepts of church life. I am more determined than ever that we shall be renewed. I am more committed to seeing the ministry and the life we share together at Our Heritage cross over all the way and once and for all into the spiritual dimension where, depending *only* on the Holy Spirit and centering *only* on the Person of Jesus, we are free to be the Body through which the Father chooses to glorify His Son in the world. Free enough from the arbitrary limitations of tradition and human scheming to be and to do together and individually whatever His plan calls for.

There are still many very tough nuts to crack, if this situation is to experience its fullest realization of itself as the Body of Christ.

When I was asked to do this writing, I protested that it was too soon.

"Give us another five years!" I said.

Assuming (and it's debatable) that the institutional church can be completely renewed without undergoing a revolution so radical as to destroy it as an institution, five years more of seeking to be open to the Spirit's work in us and on us should bring us closer to solution of such problems as:

Money

I wonder if, in five years, we will have found renewal in church money matters. We have already moved away from pledges, pressure and legalism. But we still panic when offerings fail to meet expenditures and budget commitments. And we still are not quite sure God would supply our needs if we did not publicly pass the plate.

We are learning, slowly, that this too is an area over which Christ would exercise His authority as Head of the Church. Money is such a downright practical and effective tool in His hands for discipline, chastening and guiding the work of the church, when His Lordship is recognized.

During a financial crisis period several months ago, we concluded that the church could no longer afford to hire a part-time secretary. I've been without secretarial help before, and my first fear was that I'd wind up spending precious hours doing secretarial work myself. But this time we committed the situation to the Lord and asked Him to teach us to do only those things which were really necessary and consistent with His goals and principles for the Body.

Almost immediately I discovered that much of what I had had

my secretary doing was neither necessary nor consistent. Much of it would have to be classed under "dependence on the flesh" instead of "dependence on the Spirit." And it all cost money.

This led to re-evaluation of nearly all the expenditures the church was making. Many things were found to be carry-overs from the old days of super-programming and institutionalization.

I am now convinced that ways must be found to give the Lord practical "veto power" over all church spending. This may sound archaic in the light of modern church business practices, but I wonder if working toward a "cash basis" for most church spending might not allow Him to exercise His Headship by simply not providing funds for programs and projects outside His will. In certain instances, under clear leadership of the Spirit, the Body might still decide on a step of faith that takes it beyond its visible means. But this would be the exception, not the rule.

A bigger, more expensive building should certainly be a last resort decision. Present facilities should be used fully before we allow our desire for prestige and prominence to draw us into further debt.

We have just begun our second "mother church project" in two years, using rented facilities in another part of town and commissioning families from Our Heritage to be its nucleus. We expect to repeat this in other nearby communities. This releases pressure on our facilities and soul-fellowship (koinonia) is not diluted.

If growth continues here, our next step (as the Spirit leads) is to divide the present congregation and to begin a new church right here in our immediate neighborhood. This new body would meet Sunday afternoon in our present building. It would become a full-fledged congregation in its own right, developing its own ministry and selecting its own leadership. The result: two churches of like spirit working separately and cooperately to permeate the same community . . . without the expense of additional fractionally used church buildings.

The procedure can probably be repeated until three or four congregations are using the same facilities. If we could be persuaded in our right minds[7] that God would bless Saturday meetings or Tuesday night meetings, etc., as well as Sunday meetings, the number of individual congregations using the same small facilities could, conceivably, be many more.

Budgets or other forms of decisions relating to the spending of money should be arrived at in unhurried meetings of the *whole* Body (probably as part of the Sunday services). Discussions in small groups and as a whole should encourage expression of negative feelings and doubts as well as those that are positive. After thorough discussion and plenty of time to think and pray about it, a consensus can be arrived at.

Our limited experimentation with this has produced wider involvement than the usual "business meeting" and a great deal more genuine enthusiasm and unanimity. Everyone involved felt the decisions were really his. And they were willing to give solid support to carrying them out.

Then, when funds for a project decided upon through consensus of the Body are short, the response of the church leadership is not panic or program but *prayer*. (Is it possible to imagine a church board that, instead of seeing itself as a policy-making, fund-raising body, considers every problem, financial and otherwise, on its knees in prayer and in searching of the Scriptures for God's answers?) After prayer it is taken back to the Body for reconsideration. Thus, the burden of the original decision clearly belongs to the whole fellowship, not just a few harried leaders.

It sounds slow. But it should keep the church from involvement in projects for which there is no enthusiasm in the Body, whose treasure is invariably where its *heart* is.

And the *Spirit leads* through the Body.[8]

The Sunday School Illusion

Will a half-decade more be enough to reverse the church's mistaken thinking regarding Christian education? For more than a century, the church and its parents have been deceiving them-

[7] Romans 14:5
[8] Acts 13:1-3; 15:1-29

selves. They have been living and laboring with the empty illusion that the Sunday school can and is doing the job of training their children in the fear and nurture of the Lord.

It's a lie most of us have accepted without question.

It was never part of God's perfect plan for the church that an artificial agency handle the spiritual education of children. He has a plan. His plan is 4000 years old. His plan, when put into practice, works. Our poor substitutes for His plan have not worked well even though we have mustered an impressive mountain of statistical and emotional evidence to prove otherwise. The facts are that our children are woefully lacking in both the content and practical application of God's truth.

God's plan is outlined in Deuteronomy 6:6-9. It lays the burden of teaching and training children where it belongs, in the setting where it can be done most effectively and consistently.

> These words, which I command thee this day, shall be in thine heart: And *thou* shalt teach them diligently unto thy children, and *thou* shalt talk of them when thou sittest in *thine house,* and when thou walkest by the way, and when thou liest down, and when thou risest up . . . (Italics mine.)[9]

I pray that it will not take five years for the families of Our Heritage to move away from dependence upon Sunday school for the spiritual training of our children. I will be happy to dance on its grave in sheer joy at the knowledge that Christian families are functioning as they were created to, as the primary units of spiritual life and growth of family members. I will rejoice to see Sunday school fade away because *parents* have seen the truth about its inadequacy and have taken the teaching of God's truth into their own hands and are sharing as families in worship, study, prayer and communion.

Doctrinal and Experiential Diversity

Will the day come when oneness in the Body of Christ is more than a nice devotional thought, and when there can be a genuine

[9] Also Genesis 18:19; 35:2; Deuteronomy 4:9-10; 11:18-21; 32:46-47; Exodus 10:2; 12:26-51; 13:8, 14; Joshua 24:15; 2 Timothy 1:5; 3:15; Ephesians 6:4

experience of unity and love that brings people who differ doctrinally and experientially to worship and live together in a single local congregation?

It must be possible!

Everything the Word says about the Body of Christ, the early history of that Body, says that the Church is *one*. All Christians are *one*. Those who believe the Bible teaches unconditional eternal security are *one* with those who believe the Bible teaches conditional security. Those who speak with "tongues" are *one* with those who do not — and even with those who are afraid of "speaking in tongues." Those who believe the Bible predicts a pre-tribulation Second Coming of Christ are *one* with those who believe the Second Coming will be mid or post-tribulation. Those who baptize only by immersion are *one* with those who believe that pouring or sprinkling are also Scriptural. The young long-hairs are *one* with the crew-cuts. The "street Christians" are *one* with the members of the Bible-believing institutional church. And on and on.

One . . .

Because we do not recognize it does not make it not so. "Is Christ divided?"[10]

From early days at Our Heritage, Christians I formerly would have tagged "Calvinists" and "Arminians" have worked and worshiped together, each knowing what the other believed about the security of the believer, but have refused to let it divide them even a little. In fact, each ministered in understanding and love to the other, until without changing doctrinal positions at all, those who believe the Bible teaches conditional security came to feel more secure in Christ; and those who believe the Bible teaches unconditional eternal security carefully examined their relationship with God to make sure it was real.

Our attempts to bridge the fellowship gap between "charismatic" and "non-charismatic" Christians have, on the other hand, been less successful. Some in our fellowship who "speak in tongues" and some who do not have been mature enough to be

[10] 1 Corinthians 1:13

able to appreciate each other's gifts and to experience a oneness unmarred by fear, judging, or spiritual pride. They provide a glimmer of what can and needs to develop in the future.

I cannot help but believe and hope that if Christians, whatever gifts they have or have not been given, will at least take at face value what the Bible says, they can live and work together in unity in spite of their diversity of experience. Even if they cannot agree on the level of interpretation, limited experience here in Scottsdale tells us that when they are willing to live together in First Corinthians 13, they *can* find deep and meaningful fellowship.

There must be developed somewhere the kind of church fellowship in which a person with any legitimate spiritual gift can share its blessing openly. And where the Body, instead of being fearful, jealous, or divided, will be edified in the Lord. It must be possible, in the love of Christ, for there to exist a church where the gifts of every believer (however falteringly and immature he is in his use of them) will be respected, and the ministry of even the weakest will be valued by all.

If the love we share isn't real enough to accomplish that, what good is it? According to Jesus in John 13:35, if the watching world does not see love shared by true Christians – whatever the extent of our diversity in the Lord – they have a right to conclude that we really are not Christians at all!

The Role of the Pastor

In the years ahead, the professional pastor's role must further diminish. The local church should aim to become "indigenous."

In the early church, the apostle would spend only a few months (at the most only two or three years) in a city, evangelizing and teaching. When he left, he left the local congregations in the hands of local people to whom the Spirit had given gifts and whom the apostle had appointed as "elders." These people were equipped to minister, teach, preach, lead, and to carry on all the functions needed for the growth and edification of the Body of Christ.[11] No call went out for a professional pastor *from some-*

[11] Acts 14:23; 20:17; 20:28; 1 Peter 5:1; 1 Timothy 5:17

place else to come and take the apostle's place. They were "pastored" by one of their own "elders."[12]

Wherever the Spirit is operating, He gives gifts to men. He raises up spiritual leaders, prophets, evangelists, preachers, pastors and teachers, exhorters, helpers, administrators, etc., and supplies what they need to carry on their work.[13]

My vision calls for gradually increasing dependence upon Spirit-filled men and women of our own who take over more and more of the ministry of the Word – the "pulpit ministry." At first, they would supplement the pastor's ministry. Then, as they gain experience and grow in the knowledge of the Word, I would pull back to the supplementary role, while they carry the main burden for their own church life. I would thus be released to begin other new congregations or to move into an inter-congregational ministry of the Lord's choice.

It may be that one or two of these local preachers would become so involved time-wise that they would be supported financially by the church.

It will obviously take time, and there will be adjustments to make in the thinking of both the congregation and pastor if the "indigenous church" is to be developed. But I am convinced that the ministry of a variety of gifts and persons is what the Spirit wants. Such a multiple pastoral approach would give the Spirit greater opportunity for a full-orbed ministry that can result in a more rapid and balanced process of spiritual maturity for the church.

We are involved in a perpetually unfinished task. The end of this book is an open end. It has to point to problems yet unsolved, to challenges yet unmet, to lessons not yet learned, because that is the way things are in the church in transition.

Even when we find ourselves substantially renewed, we will have to guard against drifting into a new form of establishment-

[12] Titus 1:5
[13] 1 Corinthians 12:28; Ephesians 4:11; Romans 12:6-8

arianism. Man, depending on himself, feels safer with a static organization he can learn to control. New spiritual life, however, is based on a living relationship with the Divine Person. The moment it becomes static or routine, it has become a thing man is doing, and and it is not His new *life* anymore.

There are many books being written on the subject of church renewal. Many new ideas, new methods, new formats and new structures are being suggested as "keys to renewal." Many church leaders on both the left and the right are making pronouncements on the subject.

Everyone is selling something as "the answer." Small groups. Charismatic experiences. Gospel rock. River or ocean baptism. Relational theology. Discovery games. Dialogue sermons. Personal evangelism. Social involvement. Conversational prayer. Depending on who it is to whom you are listening, any one of these (and more) might seem to be the "key to church renewal."

Doubtless if any one of these ideas would be tried in the average church, it would be like a breath of fresh air blowing through a tomb.

But . . . is a breath of fresh air enough to raise the dead?

In a recent magazine article, the president of a large Christian college declared that the antidote for "dead orthodoxy" is "evangelistic zeal." I could almost hear the thundering chorus of "amens" from all across the evangelical world.

But Jesus said, "Let the dead bury their dead"[14] . . . Nowhere did He suggest it is possible for the dead to *raise* the dead.

Evangelistic zeal arising from dead orthodoxy, at best, results in a kind of walking, pressured *death!*

The *basic* need of a church lacking renewal is not gifts or new ideas or enthusiastic leadership or freedom or love or greater knowledge of Bible doctrine or a missionary program or evangelistic zeal or even a return to New Testament organizational patterns or any of the other things I've already mentioned.

That church needs more than anything else to *know Him!*

[14] Matthew 8:22

To know *the Living Son of God.* To know the Holy Spirit. To know Him *personally.* To know Him in the power of His resurrection.[15]

If a church needs renewal, it is not primarily because it lacks dynamic leadership, or because it doesn't have revival meetings or Sunday night services anymore. The church needs renewal only because it doesn't know *Him* anymore! It has lost or nearly lost personal fellowship with *Him.* It has forgotten how to genuinely worship *Him,* as the *Person* He is. It has lost its capacity to enjoy *Him,* thank *Him,* praise *Him,* pray to *Him,* fellowship with *Him,* depend on *Him,* draw all it needs from *Him,* and have a love relationship with *Him.*

The church needing renewal tends to function as though Jesus is a historical character from 2000 years ago, the Father is austere (or permissive) and hard to reach, the Holy Spirit is referred to as "It," and the Three Persons form the Holy Trinity, which is a doctrine to argue about with cultists and liberals.

Any so-called "renewal" that does not lead the church, its leaders and its people into simple, humble, trusting relationship with the Living Jesus through His Living Spirit is *not true renewal at all.* Until a Christian or a church comes to know and trust a *"Personal Jesus,"* all attempts at revival or spiritual revitalization can only lead to a new set of institutional chains to replace the old. New life for a man or a church without seeing Christ as alive and active in their daily lives cannot be.

No church which fails to see Christ as a living, real Person, coming to us as a Personal Spirit will ever experience genuine spiritual and institutional renewal. Without the personal power of the Personal Jesus, there is no way to experience in a real sense the New Testament idea that in Christ "old things are passed away . . . all things are become new."[16]

To try to change the church in structure alone, hoping to bring renewal to it, without bringing its people to faith in the *Personal* Jesus, is as unthinkable as hoping that by removing the

[15] Philippians 3:10
[16] 2 Corinthians 5:17

wagon tongue and adding pneumatic tires the buckboard will suddenly become self-propelled.

Making Christ personal is the key to renewal. Whatever it takes to release His resurrection life in people and through people is what it will take to bring renewal.

The Holy Spirit must be seen elsewhere than in the pages of that "old, old story" in *Acts.* In genuine renewal, revival of First Century Christian experience, the Holy Spirit is *real.* He *really* speaks.[17] He *really* leads.[18] He *really* works.[19] He *really* convicts.[20] He *really* baptizes.[21] He *really* indwells.[22] He *really* equips us for ministry to the Body.[23] He *really* fills.[24] He *really* empowers.[25] He *really* comforts.[26] He *really* disciplines.[27] He *really* communicates Jesus Christ to us, and through us, to others.[28] He *really* illuminates the Word.[29] He *really* is Christ in us.[30] He *really* produces the fruit of Christ's life through us.[31] He *really* effects renewal where men count on the Living Christ.[32]

The key to renewal is whatever releases the activity of the Holy Spirit among us!

If structures hinder Him – change the structures.

If attitudes hinder Him – change the attitudes (confessing the sin involved).

If procedures, programs, patterns, forms, approaches, methods, facilities, plans, goals, or ideals hinder Him—let them be changed!

Let the irreplaceable activity of the Spirit be released.

[17] Acts 2:4; 13:2
[18] Acts 16:6, 7
[19] 1 Corinthians 12:11
[20] John 14:8-10
[21] Acts 1:5; 1 Corinthians 12:13
[22] 1 Corinthians 3:16
[23] 1 Corinthians 12:4-27
[24] Ephesians 5:18
[25] Acts 1:8; Luke 4:14
[26] John 14:26 (KJV)
[27] Hebrews 12:5-11
[28] John 15:26
[29] 1 Corinthians 2:9-12
[30] Galatians 2:20; Colossians 1:27
[31] Galatians 5:22-23
[32] 2 Corinthians 5:17

The great Old Testament renewal text, Second Chronicles 7:14 announces: *"If my people which are called by my name will humble themselves* (in recognition of the utter weakness and fruitlessness of the flesh,[33] *and pray* (as an expression of dependence on the Spirit),[34] *and seek my face* (counting everything else as loss compared to the priceless privilege of knowing the Living, Personal Jesus),[35] *and turn from their wicked ways* (repenting of all their humanism and dependence on everything but Him[36] – their sin). . . ."

That will not be renewal. But renewal will result: *"Then will I hear from heaven and will forgive their sin, and will heal their land."*

That's renewal! The activity of the Holy Spirit for us, in us, among us, and through us – forgiving our sin, healing our institutions, cleansing, setting us newly apart for His purpose, sanctifying, reviving, renewing.

Renewal can *never* be something *we are doing* to the church. It can only be what *He is doing* in the church. And, on that basis, renewal is something the church perpetually needs. For no matter how alive and vital a church may become through His doing, the very moment we assume the driver's seat, take the glory for ourselves, or even gloat over what He has done in us more than who He is among us, is the very moment it becomes *our doing,* again . . . is the very moment we need, *again,* the Holy Spirit's renewing activity!

And we will know we are there – renewed, revived, restored – when, in whatever form we congregate, we and our people fully and perfectly . . .

> . . . Know Him . . . become more deeply and intimately acquainted with Him, perceiving and recognizing and understanding (the wonders of His Person) . . . And . . . in that same way come to know the power outflowing from His resurrection (which it exerts over believers); and . . . so share His sufferings as to be continually transformed (in spirit into His likeness even) to His death. . . .

[33] John 15:5; Romans 7:18
[34] Zechariah 4:6
[35] Philippians 3:8
[36] Philippians 3:9a; Romans 14:23; Psalm 20:7

I do not consider, brethren, that I have captured *and* made it my own (yet); but one thing I do — it is my one aspiration: forgetting what lies behind and straining forward to what lies ahead, I press on toward the goal to win the (supreme and heavenly) prize to which God in Christ Jesus is calling us upward.[37]

[37] Philippians 3:10, 13, 14, *The Amplified Bible.*

APPENDIX

CAMPUS CRUSADE FOR CHRIST LAY INSTITUTE FOR EVANGELISM

Brief Suggestions for Conducting Informal Evangelistic Home Bible Studies

HOW TO BEGIN

1. Visit friends and neighbors and invite them to participate.
2. Ask friends and neighbors to invite their friends to join the group.
3. Set a definite time to meet weekly. Meetings of one hour are usually adequate.
4. Set a definite length of time such as ten weeks. Most people respond to something that doesn't seem to last forever, although most people who join your group will want to continue. . . .[1]
5. Begin and close meetings on time.
6. Choose an evening that will remain relatively free from conflicts. Tuesday or Thursday evenings are usually best.

WHAT TO SAY

"We are starting an informal Bible study in our home using this booklet (show them the introductory *Step*[2]). We'll be

[1] Our experience has been that at the end of the initial period (six, eight or ten weeks), the group will want to continue. Usually, by that time some of the group have decided to follow Christ and are anxious to go on. After becoming believers, they will want more than ever to go on as a little church, concentrating on spiritual growth and maturity.

[2] "The Uniqueness of Jesus," Introductory Step to *The Ten Basic Steps to Christian Maturity,* Dr. William R. Bright, Campus Crusade for Christ, Arrowhead Springs, San Bernardino, California.

meeting from 7:30 to 8:30 p.m. on Tuesday night for ten weeks, and we'd love to have you join us. You may feel like I used to – that I could never profit from studying the Bible, because it is such a big book and so hard to understand. However, I've learned that when a group of friends study together, it's a lot easier and a great deal of fun. The other people who will be joining us for this study are *(give names)*. We are all beginners and begin with the basics. I know you will enjoy it. Will you be able to join us?"

FIRST CLASS MEETING

1. Introduce all members as they arrive. Serve coffee to relax them. Furnish ash trays.
2. Arrange seating in a circle.
3. Explain again what you will be doing. Mention that you will try to stick to the main topic during the meetings. (This is where you will act as a guide.)
4. Provide a Bible for each person. Discuss different translations.
5. To relieve the pressure of ignorance, have all members follow as you read through the index of the *New Testament*. Then, when you ask members to turn to a particular book in the course of the study, be sure to tell *uninformed* members where to look. Example: "Turn to John 3:16. It is the fourth book of the *New Testament*. It follows Matthew, Mark and Luke. Have you found it? Now turn to the third chapter and locate verse 16." (Non-Christians usually know nothing about the Bible.)
6. Pass out introductory *Steps*. Tell members that they cost fifty cents. They usually volunteer to pay for their own. Explain briefly the contents of the booklet.
7. Turn with members to lesson one and explain how to do it. Complete several answers with them. (Leaders will find the *Teachers Manual* to the *Ten Steps* very helpful.)

SECOND CLASS MEETING (Proceed similar to above, except as follows)

1. Ask members to tell briefly about a high and low point of their week.
2. Leader may wish to comment briefly on how God uses high and low points in our lives.
3. Encourage members to invite their friends to the next meeting.

SUCCEEDING CLASS MEETINGS

1. You may wish to vary the program once or twice during the ten-week period.
   a. Play a *Uniqueness of Jesus* record by Bill Bright.
   b. Invite a sharp Christian to give his testimony (be sure it's well prepared).
2. Keep the group moving, but be careful not to overload members with so much work that they become discouraged. Remember, *their spiritual interest is limited.*
3. Plan a time during the second or third week to give the *Four Laws.*[3] Give members an opportunity to pray to invite Christ into their lives.
4. Make personal appointments with members when you sense that they need special help, and be sure you have at least one opportunity to urge them individually to receive Christ into their lives before the ten weeks are past.[4]

[3] *The Four Spiritual Laws,* a simple booklet presenting the plan of salvation and leading to a decision to receive Christ as Savior. Available from Campus Crusade for Christ, San Bernardino, California. Similar personal evangelism tools are produced by (1) The Billy Graham Evangelistic Association, 1300 Hennepin Avenue, Minneapolis, Minnesota (*Do You Know the Steps to Peace With God?*); (2) Department of Evangelism, The Wesleyan Church, Box 2000, Marion, Indiana (*Have You Heard Today's Good News?*); (3) Evangelism Division, State Missions Commission, Baptist General Convention of Texas, 302 Baptist Building, Dallas, Texas 75201 (*The Perfect Circle*); etc.

[4] Whether one makes the personal appointments as suggested or not, the Holy Spirit is going to minister the personal impact of the Word studied to the people involved in the group. Many of them will receive Christ, if it is made clear to them *how to do it.*

5. Give opportunities for conversational prayer when some members have received Christ. Discuss conversational prayer briefly at that time. Mention that prayer is just talking to God. Explain that He loves us and desires our fellowship once we come to know Him personally. Tell members that they may pray several times or not at all, as they wish. Ask them to keep prayers brief.
6. Leader will pray briefly to open meetings once prayer is introduced, or sooner, if desired. Care should be taken not to embarrass members through prayer, singing, etc.

HELPFUL SUGGESTIONS FOR GUIDING GOOD DISCUSSIONS (Summarized from list by Rev. G. Barnett)

1. Create a climate of acceptance, whatever members may do or say.
2. Create a climate where members can wrestle with their doubts.
3. To monopolists:
   a. Say, "Now let's hear from those who have not spoken."
   b. Speak to them afterwards about your problem of finding time for all to share.
4. To shy members: Ask, "What are your thoughts concerning this?"
5. Try to make sure everyone understands the points being discussed.
6. Maintain informality.
7. Encourage expression of real feelings.
8. Encourage listening without interruption.
9. Never let a member lose face.
10. To sidetrackers:
    a. Agree with some point they have made and adapt it back to the topic.
    b. Call on a sharp student who will return to the topic.
11. To the totally wrong answer:
    a. Pick out something positive and call on the rest of the group.

   b. If there is nothing positive to comment on, thank the member for sharing.
12. When several members talk at once, give priority to the shy person.
13. Summarize occasionally, as the discussion progresses.

(Taken from *Lay Trainees' Manual,* Campus Crusade for Christ, pp. 81-85.)